Afghanistan

Afghanistan

BY TERRI WILLIS

Enchantment of the World™
Second Series

Children's Press®

An Imprint of Scholastic Inc.

NEW YORK   TORONTO   LONDON   AUCKLAND   SYDNEY
MEXICO CITY   NEW DELHI   HONG KONG
DANBURY, CONNECTICUT

Frontispiece: Band-i Zulfiqar Lake, Bamyan Province

Consultant: Peter Sluglett, Professor of Middle Eastern History, University of Utah, Salt Lake City

Please note: All statistics are as up-to-date as possible at the time of publication.

Book production by Herman Adler

Library of Congress Cataloging-in-Publication Data

Willis, Terri.
  Afghanistan / by Terri Willis.
      p. cm.—(Enchantment of the world. Second series)
  Includes bibliographical references and index.
  ISBN-13: 978-0-531-18483-7
  ISBN-10: 0-531-18483-8
  1. Afghanistan—Juvenile literature. I. Title.
  DS351.5.W55 2008
  958.1—dc22   2007024175

Afghanistan

Cover photo:
Village in Hari
Rud river valley

Contents

Khyber Pass

A boy and his kite

Crossroads of a Continent

AFGHANISTAN HAS LONG BEEN A CROSSROADS. IT IS A mountainous country that lies at the heart of the western half of Asia, connecting the Middle East, South Asia, and central Asia. Ancient traders traveled across the region that is now Afghanistan, carrying silk and spices from India and China to the Mediterranean. Armies, loaded down with crossbows and canons, also trudged through its mountains.

Opposite: **A camel caravan travels down a road near the Afghan-Pakistani border.**

Entrance to the Bolan Pass from Dadur, **by James Atkinson. Atkinson traveled across Afghanistan with the British army in 1842.**

Because of its strategic central location, many civilizations tried to conquer Afghanistan. Some were successful, others were not. Over the centuries, Afghanistan has been part of many different empires and has had many rulers. Its people have experienced invasions, wars, and struggle throughout their history. They still do today.

But the Afghan people are fiercely independent. Many have tribal relations that are strong. They take pride in their accomplishments. Their knowledge of the local terrain is

Taliban fighters battled for control of Afghanistan in the 1990s.

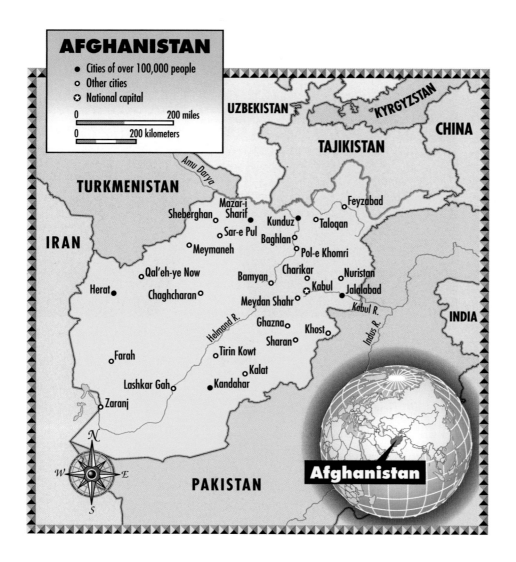

AFGHANISTAN

- ● Cities of over 100,000 people
- ○ Other cities
- ✪ National capital

0   200 miles

0   200 kilometers

UZBEKISTAN   KYRGYZSTAN

TAJIKISTAN   CHINA

TURKMENISTAN

Amu Darya

Feyzabad

Mazar-i Sharif

Sheberghan

Kunduz   Taloqan

IRAN

Sar-e Pul   Baghlan

Meymaneh   Pol-e Khomri

Qal'eh-ye Now   Charikar   Nuristan

Bamyan   Kabul   Jalalabad

Herat   Chaghcharan   Meydan Shahr

Kabul R.

Helmand R.   Ghazna   Khost

Sharan   Indus R.   INDIA

Farah   Tirin Kowt

Kalat

Lashkar Gah   Kandahar

Zaranj

N

W   E

S

PAKISTAN

Afghanistan

incomparable. They know how to use the land to their advantage, which way the wind will blow, and where the water will wash down the mountainside after it rains. They stick together and fight doggedly to maintain their lives and their freedom. So, while many have tried to conquer Afghanistan, no invader found it an easy victory.

Osama bin Laden is the leader of al-Qa'ida. The group has been responsible for a string of terrorist attacks since the 1990s.

Afghanistan's history is about more than wars, invaders, and conquerors. The country has a rich history of art, music, and religion. The people laugh, pray, eat, love, and work. Their culture has flourished, even under the pressure of war and invaders who tried to destroy it all.

Beginning in 1994, a radical religious group, the Taliban, tried to impose their conservative beliefs and practices on the country. They were successful, seizing the capital, Kabul, in September 1996.

Afghanistan came to the forefront of world news following the September 11, 2001, attacks on the United States by the extremist group al-Qa'ida. Al-Qa'ida's leader, Osama bin Laden, is from Saudi Arabia. He had to leave that country because of his harsh criticism of Saudi leaders. The Taliban allowed him into Afghanistan. By 2001, he had long been hiding out in Afghanistan's remote mountains. After the attacks, Afghan forces, with help from the United States and other countries, pushed the Taliban out of power.

Afghans held their first election in 2004, choosing new government leaders. With other countries promising money and military aid, the future looked bright for Afghanistan. Many were hopeful that their country could get on the right track, providing freedom, education, and health care to its citizens.

But in the ensuing years, much of that hope has slipped away. Many children still don't go to school or get enough to eat. Health care is poor, and violence is on the rise. And the Taliban are creeping back into power. What does the future hold for the long-suffering people of Afghanistan? Only time will tell.

Afghan women show their voting cards at a polling station north of Kabul. In 2004, Afghans elected their president directly for the first time.

A Rugged Land

Small villages are sprinkled across Afghanistan's rugged landscape.

THERE IS AN OLD STORY, TOLD BY GENERATIONS OF Afghans, about how their country came to be. According to the story, when God was nearly done creating the world, He looked at what remained—bits of rubble, unmatched pieces, leftover fragments. He gathered them up and tossed them onto the earth. Where they landed became Afghanistan.

True to this story, Afghanistan has a rough and varied landscape. It has flat plateaus and high, jagged mountains, bone-dry deserts and lush forests. There is a little bit of every kind of landscape except coast in Afghanistan.

Opposite: **Rocky, barren mountains cover much of Afghanistan.**

Fertile valleys lie amid Afghanistan's jagged mountains.

Afghanistan is a landlocked country in southwestern Asia. To the north, Afghanistan is bordered by Turkmenistan, Uzbekistan, and Tajikistan. A long, thin strip of land called the Wakhan Corridor connects Afghanistan to China in the northeast. Pakistan lies to the south and east, while Iran is to the west. Afghanistan is made up of three main regions: the northern plains, the central highlands, and the south-western lowlands.

The Northern Plains

Mountain plateaus and rolling hills make up the dry northern plains. Soil there is good for growing crops as long as water

Water in Afghanistan

Afghanistan contains a few lakes, though they are small. It also has several rivers that begin high in the mountains, where snow and glaciers melt each summer. The Amu Darya, which forms most of the country's northern border, is the longest river, at 1,578 miles (2,540 km). It is the only river in Afghanistan deep and wide enough to be used by boats. The Kabul River (below) is another important water source. It serves the farming regions near Jalalabad and Kabul in the east. The Helmand River is the main river in the southwestern part of the country. Most rivers in Afghanistan drain into lakes or simply disappear, evaporating in the desert heat. Only the Amu Darya and the Kabul flow into other rivers that eventually reach the ocean.

is available. Some enterprising farmers have diverted river water to irrigate the land. This water helps them grow rice and cotton. Other farmers raise herds of sheep and goats on the grasslands.

The Central Highlands

Mountains cover more than two-thirds of Afghanistan. The Hindu Kush mountain range dominates the central highlands. The Hindu Kush is a westward extension of the Himalayas, which contain some of the highest peaks in the world. Glaciers

Afghanistan's Geographic Features

Area: 250,775 square miles (649,504 sq km)

Greatest Distance North to South: 630 miles (1,015 km)

Greatest Distance East to West: 820 miles (1,320 km)

Bordering Countries: Turkmenistan, Uzbekistan, and Tajikistan to the north; China to the northeast; Pakistan to the east and south; Iran to the west

Highest elevation: Mount Nowshak, 24,557 feet (7,485 m) above sea level

Lowest elevation: In the Sistan Basin, 1,640 feet (500 m) above sea level

Longest River: Amu Darya, 1,578 miles (2,540 km) long

Average Annual Precipitation: 12 inches (30.5 cm)

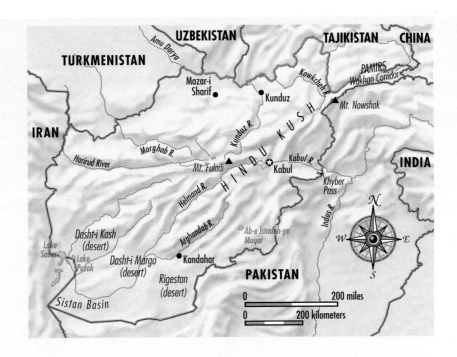

cover many peaks in the Hindu Kush. The highest peak in the range, Mount Nowshak, rises to 24,557 feet (7,485 meters) in the Wakhan Corridor. Another mountain range, the snow-capped Pamir Mountains, rises in the northeast.

Several lakes are nestled among the peaks of the Wakhan Corridor.

Rising Mountains, Shaking Earth

Earth's outer layer is split into huge pieces called tectonic plates. These plates fit together like a giant jigsaw puzzle. But unlike the pieces of a jigsaw puzzle, the tectonic plates are constantly moving. They are slowly shifting, sliding, and pushing against one another.

The mountains of Afghanistan were formed by two of these plates pressing against each other, causing the land between them to crumple and lift up. This process began many millions of years ago, and it is still happening today. The plates shift and the land wrinkles. When that happens suddenly, earthquakes occur. Massive earthquakes are common in the mountains of Afghanistan. Serious earthquakes hit the country in 1998, 2002, and 2005, killing thousands of people.

The Khyber Pass

The Khyber Pass, a twisting, challenging path that connects Afghanistan to Pakistan in the east, has played an important role in the country's history. For centuries, people have traveled the 33 miles (53 km) of the Khyber Pass through the Safed Koh range, an offshoot of the Hindu Kush mountains. One of the most accessible trails through the mountains of central Asia, it has been used by countless traders, explorers, armies, and refugees. Today, two roads run through the pass, connecting the Afghan capital, Kabul, to Peshawar, an ancient city in Pakistan. One road is for cars, trucks, and buses. Another is for the camel caravans that still make their way through the region.

Most Afghans live in the valleys of the central highlands. Some live in villages, while others live in major cities such as Jalalabad, which lie in the shadows of mountains. The nation's capital, Kabul, is located along the Kabul River in a narrow valley wedged among the mountains of the Hindu Kush. Still other Afghans, usually several related family groups, live in rural compounds known as *qal'ahs*. These are small clusters of homes built within protective walls.

Traveling in Afghanistan usually involves crossing through mountain passes. These winding, twisted paths take travelers between mountain peaks, rather than up and over them. The most important pass in Afghanistan is the Khyber Pass, which links the country to Pakistan.

The Southwestern Lowlands

The Helmand River flows from high in the Hindu Kush into the southwestern lowlands. Land along the river is good for farming. Wheat, barley, corn, and fruits are the main crops grown in the Helmand Valley. Parts of the Helmand River overflow in the spring when snow and ice high in the mountains melt. The overflow creates shallow lakes, providing temporary homes for geese, ducks, swans, plovers, larks, and other birds.

Wheat and barley are the most common legal crops grown in the Helmand Valley. Farmers in the area can make more money growing poppies, which are used to make illegal drugs.

Some of Afghanistan's most fertile lands are in the south. But so are deserts, including the Dasht-i Margo, the "Desert of Death." It got its nickname because so many people have died trying to cross it. Located in the southwest, it is the country's third-largest desert, following the Rigestan, which lies south of Kandahar, and the Dasht-i Kash, which is also in the southwest. The Rigestan is Afghanistan's sandiest desert—the others are rocky . In fact, *Rigestan* means "Country of Sand." The Rigestan's sand dunes shift constantly in the wind, at times reaching heights of 100 feet (30 m). Few roads lead through the desert, and few services are available for travelers. Most people who need to move about in Afghanistan's deserts get around by horse or camel.

Afghanistan is home to an estimated 180,000 camels. People have used camels to travel across Afghanistan for more than two thousand years.

Major Cities of Afghanistan

Afghanistan's capital, Kabul, is the nation's largest city, with 2,536,300 residents. Next largest is Kandahar, which is home to 316,000 people. Kandahar was founded in the fourth century B.C. by Alexander the Great, but excavations in the area show that humans have lived nearby for more than seven thousand years. Much of the city was destroyed in the fighting of recent decades.

Herat (right), with 249,000 people, is Afghanistan's third-largest city. It lies in the west, in the most fertile region of Afghanistan. Herat is an ancient city. In 330 B.C., it was captured by Alexander the Great. Fifteen hundred years later, Mongol invaders destroyed much of the city. Today, some ancient landmarks remain, including large earthen walls used to defend the city and the ruins of a fortress built under the direction of Alexander.

Mazar-i Sharif is Afghanistan's fourth-largest city, home to about 183,000 people. The city is famous for the lovely Blue Mosque (left). Mazar-i Sharif has traditionally been a center for the manufacture and sale of carpets, but heavy fighting in recent years has slowed business. Now, the main economic activities are agriculture and some oil and gas exploration.

Another city that has lost much of its past glory due to fighting is Jalalabad, which has 168,600 residents. Jalalabad is located in a beautiful area at the western end of the Khyber Pass. It was once a luxury resort area for the powerful. Afghanistan's last king had a palace there amid towering cypress trees. But the city endured heavy damage during the Soviet invasion (1979–1989), and the fighting has continued since then.

Much snow falls in the Hindu Kush. Ice covers the tallest peaks year-round.

The Climate

The northern and central parts of the country have a harsh climate, with severe winters. Temperatures can fall to −15 degrees Fahrenheit (−26 degrees Celsius) in the winter in the mountains. Freezing winds called scimitars howl through the mountains. Heavy snows make travel nearly impossible. Summers in these areas are sunny and warm, except at the highest elevations.

In the desert regions of the south, summers are scorching, with temperatures reaching 120°F (49°C). Some desert areas get less than 4 inches (10 centimeters) of rain per year. In the desert, strong winds blow between July and September, reaching speeds of 60 to 110 miles (97 to 177 kilometers) per hour. These fierce winds whip sand into the air, making it nearly impossible to see. Winters in the desert are generally mild.

Damage to the Land

Farmers in Afghanistan have had difficulties because only a small amount of the nation's land can be used for growing crops. But a process called desertification is making the problem even worse. Desertification is what happens when human activity turns productive land into useless desert. In Afghanistan, many people are so poor that they pull up shrubs, cut down trees, and collect animal dung to burn for warmth and cooking. These activities remove important nutrients from the soil. More damage occurs when animals are allowed to overgraze. Too many cattle strip the pastures bare of vegetation. Nothing is left to keep the soil in place, and the fertile topsoil blows away. All that remains is barren earth.

Sheep graze on meager grasses in southern Afghanistan. As the land is stripped of plants, the deserts expand.

Even worse environmental damage comes from land mines. These are weapons that are buried just under the ground. They are supposed to explode when a military vehicle drives over them, but they also go off if a person or an animal steps on them. Millions of land mines have been buried in Afghanistan since 1979. In that year, Afghanistan was invaded by the Soviet Union, a huge country composed of Russia and other now-independent nations in eastern Europe and central Asia. First, Soviet forces, who occupied Afghanistan for a decade, mined the land heavily. Later, various Afghan forces also laid mines. They each needed to protect their main supply routes. This meant that mines were particularly heavy along the road north from Kabul to the border and around airports and major cities.

Land mines continue to cause many deaths in Afghanistan. They have forced more than a million farmers to abandon their plots and nomadic animal herders to give up their traditional way of life.

Some organizations are working to try to make the land safe again. One such group, the HALO Trust, works in several countries where land mines are a problem, including Afghanistan. Removing the mines is painstaking work, which must be done slowly and carefully to ensure that there are no injuries. Sometimes, machines can do the work. Other times, humans, well protected with body armor, remove the mines. When an area is cleared, it is marked, often with something as simple as painted rocks. White rocks mean it is safe, red rocks signal danger.

Since HALO began work in Afghanistan in 1988, it has cleared more than five million land mines and other exploding weapons and booby traps. But many more remain. If work does not continue, the country will suffer thousands more land-mine deaths in the coming decades.

A man uses a metal detector to search for land mines. Afghanistan is one of the most heavily mined countries in the world.

A Tough Environment

P LANTS AND ANIMALS HAVE IT TOUGH IN AFGHANISTAN. In the northern part of the country, temperatures can be both extremely hot and extremely cold. In the mountains, cold, strong winds whip across the landscape. In the south lie hot, dry, dusty deserts. Few living things can thrive in these conditions. Only hardy plants and animals survive Afghanistan's challenging environments.

Opposite: **Cherry trees bloom on the outskirts of Kabul.**

The hardy pindrow fir grows in the mountains of Afghanistan.

Plants

Afghanistan's mountains are generally treeless. In fact, less than 3 percent of the nation's land is forested. Most trees have been cut down either for firewood or to use as timber. In many places, only scrub bushes and thick grasses grow. But high on some mountains, dense forests of cedar, pine, and fir still cover the land. Farther down the slopes, walnut, hazel, oak, acacia, and wild peach trees grow. Shrubs such as wormwood, camel thorn, locoweed, and mimosa also thrive there. Flowers blooming on these mountainsides include wild rose and honeysuckle.

In the deserts, the only trees are date palms. Grassy plants and small shrubs grow in the sand dunes. Their long roots tap into deep reserves of water and help hold the soil in place during heavy winds. These plants usually grow some distance from one another, so that each gets enough water. Often, the desert plants have small, waxy leaves. As a result, they don't lose as much moisture from their pores as other plants do. During the cooler, wetter times of the year, these plants store nutrients in their roots. This helps them survive when the weather turns hot and dry.

In much of Afghanistan, only the toughest shrubs survive.

Trees in the Desert

Date palms are the only trees that can survive in the Afghan desert. They grow sparsely in oases, where some water is available. A single date palm tree produces up to 600 pounds (270 kilograms) of fruit. At one time, the Afghan desert was home to many nomads, who traveled in search of resources. The nomads depended on date palms for their survival.

In more fertile areas, some herbs, such as mint, grow wild. Farmers raise vegetables, including peas, onions, turnips, cabbages, cucumbers, and artichokes. Fruits such as bananas, peaches, grapes, and strawberries are also grown. Other farmers cultivate such grains as wheat, rice, barley, and corn. North of the Hindu Kush, pistachio trees are common. Their nuts are gathered and sold.

Onions are one of the many vegetables that grow well in eastern Afghanistan.

Markhors are notable for their thick, spiraling horns. The horns on male markhors can grow more than 60 inches (150 cm) long.

Animals

More than one hundred species of mammals live in Afghanistan, though some of them are nearly extinct. Snow leopards, antelope, gazelles, deer, and wolves are among the largest mammals in the country. Others include boars, mark-hors (a type of large goat), hyenas, jackals, Afghan foxes, and mongooses. Hares, hedgehogs, jerboas, shrews, and bats are among the smaller mammals.

Reptiles and amphibians in Afghanistan include a variety of snakes, lizards, skinks, salamanders, and frogs. There are many species of freshwater fish in the nation's rivers, streams, and lakes, especially trout.

Common domesticated animals include cattle, sheep, and goats, each raised for its milk and meat. Afghans also keep horses and donkeys for transportation. Some camels are found in Afghanistan. The one-humped dromedary camel works on the plains, while the two-humped Bactrian camel is used in the mountains.

McMahon's viper is one of the 109 known reptile species in Afghanistan. It lives in dry areas of western Afghanistan.

The Karakul Sheep

In the northern highlands of Afghanistan, near the banks of the Amu Darya, lives a breed of sheep called the Karakul. The Karakul were domesticated at least 3,500 years ago. They were likely the first breed of sheep to be domesticated. Well suited to the highlands' rough climate, Karakul sheep store fat in their large tails to use for nourishment later, in much the same way that camels store fat in their humps. This enables Karakul sheep to survive even in periods of drought, when there isn't much to eat.

Karakul sheep are known for their fine wool. Their fleece has little grease, so it spins easily into yarn. The yarn is of high quality and is woven into carpets, saddle blankets, and cloaks.

More than four hundred species of birds have been found in Afghanistan, including partridges, pheasants, and woodcocks. Some, such as the Siberian crane, were widely hunted and are now rare. Afghanistan is an important route for many birds traveling south from Siberia, in northern Asia, to India, in southern Asia, for the winter. In recent decades, persistent warfare has prevented the birds from stopping in their favorite resting places on their long journey. As a result, flocks get split up, some birds get lost and die, and others die of stress. Pelicans, flamingos, geese, swans, and ducks are all at risk.

Some bar-headed geese breed in the lakes of northeastern Afghanistan. They are thought to fly higher than any other birds as they migrate from India over the Himalayas to their breeding grounds.

Traders and Invaders

36

THE HISTORY OF AFGHANISTAN STRETCHES ACROSS THOUsands of years. The nation sits on the path of an important ancient trade route. But long before there were traders or nations, there were hunters. Some one hundred thousand years ago, prehistoric people stalked prey through the northern foothills of the Hindu Kush.

Thousands of years later, people developed farming skills. They herded animals and grew wheat and barley on the plateaus and in the valleys. Over time, the farmers gathered into small villages, which evolved into small cities by about 4000 B.C. They traded grains, cotton, and pottery with people in the regions that are now Egypt, Iraq, and India.

In about 1500 B.C., a group of nomadic warriors called the Aryans moved into the Afghan region from central Asia. They settled on the north-central plains, then called Bactria and now known as Balkh. The Aryans spoke many languages. Two of them—Dari and Pashto—

Opposite: **Afghans inspect goods at a market in Kabul.**

A farmer gathers beans near Bamyan, Afghanistan.

are still spoken today. They are Afghanistan's national languages. The Aryans were good farmers and organized effective governments. They had a strong empire for nearly a thousand years.

Cyrus the Great conquered the area that is now Afghanistan in the sixth century B.C. In this painting from A.D. 1475, he is shown as a medieval king.

Early Conquests

In the sixth century B.C., Cyrus the Great ruled the Achaemenid Empire in Persia (now Iran). He had his army take over the fertile Bactria region to expand his empire. This was the start of Afghanistan's history of invasion and conquest. Forty years later, the son of Cyrus, Darius I, brought all of what is now Afghanistan into the Achaemenid Empire.

About two hundred years later, the Achaemenid Empire lost its hold on the region. At that time, Alexander the Great, a Macedonian from the area just north of Greece, was a great empire-building warrior. He was attracted by the bounty of Afghanistan and the fact that it was the gateway to India. In 329 B.C., his troops took over Herat in the west. In two years, they had added all of Afghanistan to their empire.

After Alexander the Great's death in 323 B.C., three of his top generals fought for power. They split Alexander's empire. One of the generals, Seleucus, founded the Seleucid dynasty, which included most of northern Afghanistan.

During the same period, Chandragupta Maurya, a ruler in northern India, led an army to take over the region south of the Hindu Kush. He established the Mauryan dynasty there. The Mauryan dynasty developed an organized government with many new

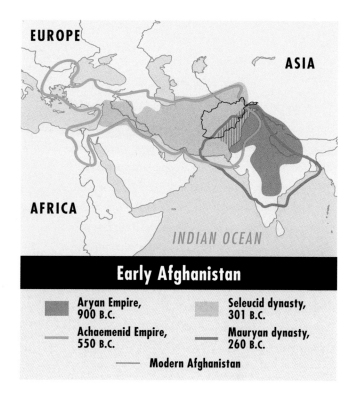

Early Afghanistan

- Aryan Empire, 900 B.C.
- Achaemenid Empire, 550 B.C.
- Seleucid dynasty, 301 B.C.
- Mauryan dynasty, 260 B.C.
- Modern Afghanistan

ideas. The government collected taxes and built irrigation systems. These enabled farmers to grow enough crops to trade with people from other areas. Chandragupta also set up a standard system of weights and measures, which helped people trade goods easily.

The Buddhist religion took hold in the Afghanistan region during the Mauryan dynasty. Faithful followers built shrines filled with beautiful sculptures. Buddhism continued to spread as travelers and traders made their way to and from India, China, and central Asia.

No group was more influential in the spread of Buddhism at this time than the Kushan, who came from central Asia to rule over a region that includes much of present-day Afghanistan, Pakistan, and India. They made Buddhism the official religion of their dynasty.

The Silk Road

From about the second century B.C., the major trade route across Asia was the Silk Road. It wound for about 5,000 miles (8,000 km) between China, India, and the Mediterranean Sea. People transported silk, jewelry, spices, pottery, and more along the route.

Afghanistan was at the heart of the Silk Road. The largest trading depot along the route was in Bactra (now Balkh, Afghanistan), and Afghanistan's Amu Darya, a river known in ancient times as the Oxus, was an important part of the Silk Road. Afghanistan's major trade item, a blue semiprecious stone called lapis lazuli, is still found today in mines along the river.

The Silk Road

— Land trade route   ● Trade center

— Sea trade route   Modern Afghanistan

The Kushan dynasty was successful for about three hundred years, until the middle of the third century A.D. Then, the Sasanians from the north conquered part of the dynasty's holdings. The Sasanians held power in southwestern Asia for some four hundred years.

Arab Armies Invade

In 642, Arab armies spreading the religion of Islam invaded Afghanistan from the west. Islam had begun in the city of Mecca, in what is now Saudi Arabia. In 632, Arab armies headed out from Arabia, in an effort to convert more people to Islam. By 642, they entered what is now Afghanistan. By the early 700s, all of Afghanistan was under Arab rule.

Arab control of Afghanistan lasted until 920. The new conquerors were also Muslims, followers of Islam. Called the Samanids, they came from the north to control a large region that included present-day Afghanistan, India, and Iraq. But their reign was short. In Persia, Turkish slave-soldiers staged an uprising. They overthrew their Samanid masters, and the Ghaznavid dynasty was born.

The Ghaznavid dynasty takes its name from the magnificent city of Ghazna, the center of the dynasty's power and its capital. The Ghaznavid dynasty lasted until 1150, when it was conquered by the Ghurids, who had come from the mountains near Herat. Here, the Ghurids established their capital. The Ghurids burned down Ghazna. Today, little remains of its former glory. The Ghurids' reign lasted little more than half a

Mahmud of Ghazna

Mahmud of Ghazna, the third of the Ghaznavid dynasty's rulers, is often considered the greatest of all ancient Afghan leaders. Born in 971, he ruled from 998 to 1030. Mahmud transformed Ghazna into a showplace of culture. Poets, musicians, and artists gathered there under Mahmud's support. The city was filled with marble mosques, lavish gardens, and fine schools.

Mahmud was also a great military strategist. He led armies that took control of lands stretching from western Persia to the Ganges River in India. Through these conquests, he converted many people to Islam. In this picture, Mahmud is depicted at the far right greeting officials from India.

century. They and their empire were crushed by a devastating force—Genghis Khan and the Mongols.

Mongol Rule

Genghis Khan was born with the name Temujin in the 1100s near the border of present-day Russia and Mongolia. After he rose to power, Mongol leaders branded him Genghis Khan, meaning "universal monarch" or, basically, "ruler over all." In 1219, he and his Mongol army invaded Afghanistan. Their destructive occupation lasted just eight years, but it erased hundreds of years of progress. It would take the Afghans centuries more to recover from the damage.

Genghis Khan became one of the most famous and dreaded conquerors in history. His empire—the world's largest—

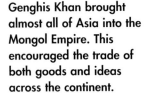

Genghis Khan brought almost all of Asia into the Mongol Empire. This encouraged the trade of both goods and ideas across the continent.

The Ruthless Genghis Khan

Genghis Khan was ruthless. His armies waged war with a kind of havoc never seen before. The devastation in Afghanistan was particularly severe. The Mongols' first stop was the capital city of Herat, where they killed nearly everyone. They slaughtered animals, chopped down orchards, and turned buildings to rubble. Then they moved on to the city of Balkh, along the Amu Darya, where they emptied Balkh's library of its priceless manuscripts and dumped them in the river. The Mongols also spread salt over farmland and plowed it in, so that nothing could grow. They filled wells and irrigation canals with sand so that people could not get water. When the Mongols came to Afghanistan, little was spared.

stretched from China to the Adriatic Sea in Europe. It covered nearly the entire Asian continent.

After Genghis Khan's death in 1227, other Mongol rulers took charge, but none had the forceful personality needed to control such a vast empire. No one was truly in charge for the next one hundred years.

The people of Afghanistan slowly began to rebuild. But in 1369, another Mongol conqueror, Timur, took control. A distant descendant of Genghis Khan, he also caused great destruction throughout the land.

Timur had a intellectual side as well. He enjoyed culture and supported poets and sculptors. During his rule, art and literature were reborn, and beautiful buildings went up. This was the beginning of the Great Timurid Era, one of the richest periods in Afghanistan's long history. Trade flourished, and cities in Afghanistan prospered. Religious schools, called *madrasas*, were built, along with shrines and mosques.

Timur was both a cold-blooded warrior and a great patron of the arts.

Babur founded the Mughal Empire, which was based in India. He was a descendant of both Genghis Khan and Timur.

The Mughal Empire

In 1504, the Great Timurid Era came to an end. Babur, the founder of the Mughal Empire, conquered Kabul. Babur made his mark in the region as a military expert. Though his armies were strong, Babur made sure that they were honorable. He did not allow his troops to harm innocent people or steal from those they conquered.

Babur loved the city of Kabul and made it his headquarters. From there, he planned his conquest of the Indian city of Delhi, which became the Mughal capital for the next three hundred years. Babur moved to India but visited Kabul when he could. Known as the "Prince of Gardeners," he enjoyed landscaping and growing local plants. After his death in 1530, he was buried in a tomb in one of his Kabul gardens.

After Babur's death, Afghanistan remained part of the Mughal Empire, but the Safavid Empire, based in Persia, was also interested in Afghanistan. The Safavids and the Mughals battled for Afghanistan for two hundred years. Boundaries moved often, and cities frequently changed hands.

Meanwhile, much of the actual power in Afghanistan was held by leaders of some 350 separate tribes scattered throughout the countryside. Eventually, the Pashtuns emerged as the strongest tribe. They lived in the mountainous region that lies at what is today the border between Afghanistan and Pakistan. In the early 1700s, a group of Pashtuns took over much of the region.

Afghanistan, 1500–1800

Mughal Empire, 1701	—— Durrani dynasty, 1772
Safavid Empire, 1722	—— Modern Afghanistan

The Durrani Dynasty

After about thirty years, an army led by Nadir Shah, the ruler of Iran, conquered Afghanistan. But in 1747, Nadir Shah was assassinated by his bodyguards, whose commander was a Pashtun, Ahmad Khan Abdali Durrani. Slowly, Durrani gained power. He eventually became the shah, or leader, of Afghanistan and was called Ahmad Shah Durrani. His ultimate goal was to make Afghanistan an independent country.

This was not easy. The many ethnic tribes of Afghanistan were used to being independent of central control. They often fought one another and had little interest in uniting. Ahmad Shah Durrani worked hard to earn the respect and trust of the tribal leaders. He convinced them that they would be stronger and better off as a unified force. But he also compromised, allowing each chief to handle his own tribe's internal affairs.

Ahmad Shah united the country and established the Durrani dynasty. Its domain stretched from India to Persia and from the Amu Darya to the Arabian Sea. It was the second-largest Muslim empire at the time. Later, Ahmad Shah became known as the "Father of Afghanistan."

Timur Shah took over when his father died in 1772. He moved Afghanistan's capital to Kabul, where it remains today. After his death in 1793, no clear leader followed. Rival Pashtun tribes battled for control of Afghanistan until 1826, when Dost Muhammad Khan emerged as the new leader.

Dost Muhammad Khan fled Afghanistan when the British invaded in 1839. He returned in 1842 and negotiated peace with the British.

The Great Game

Dost Muhammad's father had been murdered by the Durrani tribe, and he wanted revenge. He defeated his opponents and named himself emir, or prince, of Afghanistan.

Both the British and the Russians wanted control of Afghanistan. The Russians thought it would help give them access to ports on the Indian Ocean. The British wanted Afghanistan to serve as a buffer between the Russians and British territory in India. Britain was also threatened by Russia's expansion of its empire into central Asia.

The British captured Ghazna during the Second Anglo-Afghan War. The war lasted from 1878 until 1880.

Afghanistan was caught in the middle of the struggle between these two powerful nations. And Dost Muhammad was about to make matters worse.

In an effort to increase the size of his empire, Dost Muhammad declared war on Ranjit Singh, the ruler of the Punjab, a region on what is now the India-Pakistan border. Dost Muhammad needed help to conquer the Punjab. He first approached the British, but they refused. The British wanted the Punjab for themselves. Then Dost Muhammad asked the Russians for help. This enraged the British, and they invaded Afghanistan in 1839. This was the beginning of a series of bloody wars between Afghanistan, Great Britain, and Russia that became known as "the Great Game."

The Durand Line

One border drawn during Sirdar Abdur Rahman Khan's reign is known as the Durand Line. It is the boundary between Afghanistan and a former part of India that is now Pakistan. In 1893, the British drew the Durand Line, which runs right through the Hindu Kush. The line made sense in that it turned Afghanistan into a buffer zone between Russian-controlled areas and British-Indian-controlled areas. But it caused problems because it split the traditional homeland of the Pashtun tribe. The Pashtuns have great loyalty to one another, yet the Durand Line put them in two different nations that are sometimes in conflict. The Durand Line continues to create problems today, as Pashtuns are often forced to choose between their country and their tribe.

Eventually, Britain and Afghanistan would fight three wars. The First Anglo-Afghan War began in 1839, when British forces captured Ghazna, Kandahar, and Kabul and set up a new Afghan government. The Afghans rebelled, fighting until the British retreated down the Khyber Pass into what is now Pakistan.

The Second Anglo-Afghan War began in 1878. Dost Muhammad's son, Sher Ali Khan, was now the Afghan leader. He invited a Russian delegation to Kabul, but he denied British diplomats entry. This infuriated the British, who invaded Afghanistan in retaliation. Sher Ali fled the country and died a year later. His son Yaqub was the next Afghan leader. He signed a treaty with the British, enabling the rulers of British India to control Afghanistan's foreign affairs.

Yaqub resigned soon after. His cousin Sirdar Abdur Rahman Khan ruled from 1880 until his death in 1901. During this time, he set up a national court system, improved the military, and helped establish official borders for the country. For the first time, Afghanistan took the shape that it has today.

Afghanistan. Afghan traders could no longer make their way through Pakistan to India.

Unable to do business with India, Afghanistan turned to the Soviet Union for help. The Soviet Union responded by buying all of Afghanistan's harvest for the year. Afghanistan was grateful for its assistance, but Zahir Shah didn't want to be dependent on this kind of aid. In 1953, he appointed his cousin Mohammad Daoud as prime minister, specifically to improve Afghanistan's economy.

In the last century, the laws governing the clothing and education of Afghan women have repeatedly shifted.

Together, Zahir Shah and Daoud improved conditions in Afghanistan. Education was expanded, and the army was strengthened. Women were again free to show their faces in public. But Daoud resigned in 1963, after stirring up tensions with Pakistan over the Pashtun issue.

Zahir Shah continued to modernize Afghanistan. In 1964, he approved a new constitution that gave citizens greater rights to free speech and to elect their own officials. He allowed new political parties to form, including the People's Democratic Party of Afghanistan (PDPA), a communist group closely tied to the Soviet Union. Women even gained the right to vote.

But this all backfired when the newly elected representatives disagreed with Zahir Shah on many ideas. He tried to pull back on some of the new freedoms, but this angered Afghans.

Then, a severe drought hit the country in the early 1970s, causing some one hundred thousand deaths, and Zahir Shah lost even more support. In 1973, while Zahir Shah was out of the country, Daoud staged a coup, or takeover, of the throne.

The April Revolution

Daoud ruled Afghanistan for five years. During that time, he turned his back on the Soviet Union, which had been providing aid to the country. Instead, he began to ally with Saudi Arabia and Iran. The extreme religious conservatives he appointed to government positions shared his anti-Soviet views.

This upset some Afghan military leaders who supported the Soviets. These leaders, along with former members of the PDPA, assassinated Daoud in April 1978. This coup became known as the April Revolution.

The new government put Soviet-style communist policies in place. Its members proposed education for all, and land reforms to help poor people. But they also employed harsh tactics against those who disagreed. Thousands of Muslim religious leaders were imprisoned, and many were killed.

Muhammad Daoud worked to improve Afghanistan's economy. He also grabbed a lot of power for himself and his friends and did not allow any political parties but his own.

It didn't take long for the Afghans to rise up in revolt, but the situation was chaotic. In December 1979, Soviet forces invaded to try to put down the revolt. The Soviets installed Babrak Karmal as president.

The Soviet military kept about 120,000 troops in Afghanistan to make sure the Karmal government was successful. But unrest continued. Most Afghans opposed the Soviets. Men formed groups of fighters, known as the *mujahidin*. These groups would fight the Soviets for the next ten years.

Soviet tanks rolled into Afghanistan in 1979. They stayed for a decade.

The Mujahidin

The mujahidin were a loosely knit group of men from various Afghan tribes. They were later assisted by Muslim extremists from other countries who wanted to fight the Soviet occupation of Afghanistan. The mujahidin saw the occupation as a grave threat not only to Afghanistan's independence but also to Islam. They declared a *jihad*, or "holy war." In fact, the word *mujahidin* means "those fighting a Muslim holy war."

The mujahidin didn't have the weapons to stage massive attacks. Instead, they frustrated the Soviets with smaller raids and offensives. They damaged roads and destroyed Soviet communication systems. They seized buildings and murdered Soviet officials. Because many of the mujahidin fighters had grown up in the mountains of Afghanistan, they knew how to get around the rugged terrain. They knew the caves, the tunnels, the rivers. They could hide and were skilled at surviving in the harsh mountain weather. The mujahidin launched many attacks from mountain hideouts.

The mujahidin eventually gained the support of the United States, China, Saudi Arabia, and Iran.

These countries supplied them with weapons and other military supplies. With the help of these nations, the mujahidin slowly forced the Soviets to withdraw.

The Soviet Union did massive damage to Afghanistan. Soviet forces blew up irrigation systems. They destroyed forests, burned crops, and massacred animals. About one million Afghans were killed during the ten-year war. Another five or six million fled the country. Most went to Pakistan and Iran.

The mujahidin were poorly armed and at first were not able to mount a strong resistance. Then, after about five years, other nations became involved in the conflict. The United States, long an enemy of the Soviet Union, gave the mujahidin weapons and training. When China, Iran, and Saudi Arabia also began assisting the mujahidin, the tide in the war turned. In 1986, the Karmal government was forced out. The war had become very expensive for the Soviet Union, and few people in the Soviet Union supported it. In 1989, the Soviet Union withdrew its troops from Afghanistan.

The mujahidin continued to fight the Afghan government, finally toppling it in 1992. This victory did not bring peace, however. Various tribes still battled each other, and different groups of mujahidin fought among themselves. With no strong national leadership, Afghanistan was again consumed by civil war. Kidnappings, rape, and murder were common. Out of this disorder, a new group promising peace emerged. These were Islamic fundamentalists called the Taliban.

The Rise of the Taliban

The Taliban first came on the scene around 1994. Many Taliban had been students at conservative religious schools where they learned a strict version of Islam. They had fled the Soviet invasion and ended up in refugee camps in the Pashtun region along the Afghanistan-Pakistan border. The Taliban took the conservative ideals they had been taught even further. Led by a *mullah*, or Islamic cleric, named Muhammad Omar, they planned to bring peace to their country by enforcing strict religious customs.

Rules of the Taliban

The Taliban took over Kabul in September 1996. Shortly afterward, they announced sixteen decrees. These rules listed activities that were no longer allowed. The decrees included:

- Prohibition of "female exposure." If a woman is seen not wearing a *chadri* (full-body veil), her husband will be punished.
- Prohibition of music. If a music tape is found in a vehicle, the driver will go to prison.
- Prohibition of shaving. Any man without a beard must go to prison until his beard is the length of a clenched fist.
- Prohibition of kite flying. Kite flying leads to truancy, the death of children, and gambling, and is not allowed.
- Prohibition of gambling. Gamblers will go to prison for one month.
- Prohibition of washing clothes by riverbanks. The husbands of women who break this rule will be severely punished.
- Prohibition of photographs and portraits. Since only God can create anything that looks alive, those who have photos of people and animals will be punished.
- Prohibition of tailors making clothes for women. If fashion magazines are found in a tailor's shop, the tailor will be imprisoned.

The Taliban opposed the mujahidin and tried to end fighting among various tribes. They took away guns and punished criminals severely. Initially, many Afghans appreciated the peace and supported the Taliban. But the peace they provided came with a price. There were many rules to follow, and those who disobeyed often had their hands or feet cut off, or worse. Under the Taliban, girls were not supposed to be educated, and many schools shut down.

Slowly, the Taliban gained hold of Afghanistan. By 1996, they controlled Kabul, and they soon took over most of the country.

The Taliban had money to enforce their goals, in part because of Osama bin Laden. Much of the world had not yet heard of bin Laden when he moved to Afghanistan in 1996. Bin Laden led a group of fighters called al-Qa'ida. Their ultimate goal was to unite all Muslims under one strict Islamic government. The goals of al-Qa'ida meshed well with those of the Taliban, and the Taliban gave bin Laden and his followers a safe place to live. In return, bin Laden, who came

The Bamyan Buddhas

In March 2001, the Taliban angered people throughout the world when they blew up the Bamyan Buddhas, two large statues carved into the hills near Bamyan. More than 1,500 years old, these statues were international treasures. The Taliban said that they were destroyed because the statues were idols that might be worshipped by non-Muslims.

from an extremely wealthy Saudi family, shared millions of dollars with the Taliban.

The Taliban's main opposition was called the Northern Alliance. The group was led by Ahmad Shah Mas'ud, who had served as the Afghan defense minister after the Soviets left. The Northern Alliance slowed the Taliban advance throughout Afghanistan, though ultimately the Taliban prevailed. Still, the Northern Alliance continued to fight.

Ahmad Shah Mas'ud

Many consider Ahmad Shah Mas'ud Afghanistan's greatest modern hero. His photo hangs in homes, in shops, and on streets throughout the country.

Born in 1953, Mas'ud was an ethnic Tajik who studied engineering at Kabul University. While in college in 1972, he joined a Muslim student group opposed to the communist influence that was taking hold in Afghanistan. Later, as a military leader, he helped run the Soviets out of Afghanistan. In the early 1990s, he became Afghan defense minister, but he lost that job when the Taliban came to power. In response, he organized the Northern Alliance and led them in their fight against the Taliban.

On September 9, 2001, Mas'ud was assassinated in Afghanistan by two al-Qa'ida agents posing as journalists. Al-Qa'ida's Saudi leader, Osama bin Laden, probably ordered his death. A few months later, the new Afghan president, Hamid Karzai, awarded Mas'ud the title "Hero of the Afghan Nation."

His tomb, a simple structure in the Panjshir Valley northeast of Kabul, is a popular place for Afghans to visit.

September 2001

Many things changed in September 2001. On September 9, Mas'ud was assassinated, likely by al-Qa'ida agents. This was big news in Afghanistan but not elsewhere.

Then, on September 11, 2001, two passenger planes were crashed into the towers of the World Trade Center in New York City. Another plane was flown into the Pentagon in Washington, D.C. A fourth plane crashed into a field in Pennsylvania. More than three thousand people lost their lives that day. Most were inside the World Trade Center towers, skyscrapers that burned and then collapsed to the ground.

The four planes had been hijacked by members of al-Qa'ida. The United States retaliated less than a month later by unleashing cruise missiles on Afghanistan. Their targets were al-Qa'ida training camps and the Taliban. Soon, soldiers from the United States and other nations were on the ground in Afghanistan, working with Northern Alliance forces. It took them only a few months to defeat the Taliban. Some Taliban surrendered. Others fled or went into hiding. But neither Osama bin Laden nor Mullah Omar was captured.

Terrorists crashed airliners into the twin towers of the World Trade Center on the morning of September 11, 2001. In less than two hours, both towers collapsed.

By December, an interim government was in place, headed by Hamid Karzai. A few months later, in June 2002, the country held a *loya jirga*, or "great assembly," to select a new president. It was made up of 1,501 delegates from throughout the country. They represented many different ethnic groups, and even women participated. The loya jirga was a success. Karzai was named president, and a transitional government was set up.

Hamid Karzai was born into a prominent family in Kandahar. His political activity began in the 1980s, when he joined the struggle against the Soviets.

An Uncertain Future

The lives of Afghan citizens began to return to normal. Schools reopened, and girls could attend. People listened to music and flew kites, and women were free to leave their homes without wearing chadris. Slowly, life was getting better.

Afghanistan held its first democratic elections ever in 2004. About one-third of the people—more than eight million citizens—registered to vote, including about 40 percent of eligible women. The Taliban had threatened to interrupt the vote and to attack participants, but the election was fairly peaceful. Hamid Karzai was elected president.

Meanwhile, the Taliban fought to retake the country. Bombings became more common. Troops from several countries, including the United States, remained in Afghanistan, fighting the Taliban and trying to rebuild. But the number of American troops in Afghanistan declined as the United States pulled them out of Afghanistan to fight the war in Iraq.

In early 2007, the Taliban stepped up its attacks, targeting civilians and the military. The U.S. military responded by increasing its attacks on the Taliban. But the number of Afghan civilians accidentally killed by U.S. bombs rose. Afghans, after decades of war, were weary.

In an effort to halt the fighting, the Afghan parliament began considering plans to have foreign troops withdraw. They also considered negotiating with the Taliban, bringing them into the government. What will become of these plans? The future of Afghanistan remains uncertain.

U.S. troops search for Taliban fighters in 2003. Though the Taliban had been ousted in 2002, they were regaining power by 2007.

Striving for Stability

AFGHANISTAN'S PEOPLE ARE STRUGGLING TO STABI-lize their country. This is difficult, as the country remains in turmoil. The central government has little control in many parts of Afghanistan. Instead, tribal warlords hold power, and the Taliban are also reasserting themselves.

Opposite: **The Taliban continue to battle for control of Afghanistan.**

The Constitution

The shape of Afghanistan's government was set in its newest constitution, which was approved in 2004. According to the constitution, Afghanistan is an Islamic republic with three branches of government—executive, legislative, and judicial. In addition, the constitution calls for a loya jirga, or "great assembly," which meets under certain conditions. The country is divided into thirty-four provinces, each led by a provincial governor. Many of these governors are former warlords who are not really dependent on or responsible to the central government in Kabul.

President Hamid Karzai addresses the loya jirga in 2003.

Children perform at the end of Afghanistan's constitutional convention in January 2004. Delegates worked for weeks to come up with a constitution acceptable to the nation's many different ethnic groups.

The Executive Branch

Afghanistan's constitution calls for a strong executive branch. The head of the executive branch is the president. The people of Afghanistan elect the president. If no candidate earns at least 50 percent of the vote, the two candidates with the most votes take part in a second election.

The executive branch also includes two vice presidents and members of the cabinet. Cabinet ministers are appointed by the president but must be approved by the National Assembly.

Afghanistan's National Anthem

Afghanistan's 2004 constitution established rules for choosing a new national anthem: The anthem must be in the Pashto language; it must contain the phrase "Allah Akbar," meaning "God is great"; and it must include the names of all of Afghanistan's ethnic groups. President Hamid Karzai approved the new national anthem in 2006.

> This land is Afghanistan. It is the pride of every Afghan.
> The land of peace, the land of the sword. Its sons are all brave.
> This is the country of every tribe—land of the Baluch, and the Uzbeks,
> Pashtuns, and Hazaras—Turkman and Tajiks with them,
> Arabs and Gojars, Pamirian, Nuristanis,
> Barahawi, and Qizilbash. Also Aimaq, and Pashaye.
> This land will shine forever, like the sun in the blue sky.
> In the chest of Asia, it will remain as the heart forever.
> We will follow the one God. We all say, Allah is great, we all say,
> Allah is great.

The Legislative Branch

Afghanistan's legislative branch, the National Assembly, is a two-house parliament. The upper house, the House of Elders, has 102 members. Two-thirds are elected by local councils from each of Afghanistan's thirty-four provinces. The other one-third is appointed by the president. At least half of the appointed members must be women. Two must be disabled, and two more must be nomads. Members of the House of Elders must be at least thirty-five years old. Appointed members serve for five-year terms, while the others serve for three or four years.

NATIONAL GOVERNMENT OF AFGHANISTAN

Executive Branch

PRESIDENT

VICE PRESIDENTS

CABINET

Legislative Branch

HOUSE OF ELDERS   HOUSE OF THE PEOPLE

Judicial Branch

SUPREME COURT

APPEAL COURTS

HIGH COURTS

Malalai Joya

One of the strongest voices speaking out for the rights of women in Afghanistan in recent years has belonged to Malalai Joya, the youngest member of Afghanistan's parliament. Her voice may be quieted though, since in May 2007 Joya was suspended from the parliament for three years.

Joya was elected to the House of the People in 2005, when she was twenty-seven years old. Immediately, she campaigned for women's rights, making sure women's needs were represented within the government. This angered some people in the country, especially those who feel that women don't deserve equal rights. In the space of little more than a year she had survived four assassination attempts. "They will kill me," she told one journalist, "but they will not kill my voice, because it will be the voice of all Afghan women. You can cut the flower but you cannot stop the coming of spring."

Her task was difficult. "Life is as bad, if not worse," she said in a speech to her colleagues in parliament in May 2006. "There continue to be no women's rights in Afghanistan. In some provinces they ban schools for women and publish leaflets warning them not to go." After her speech, some members of parliament threw bottles at her. Joya has six bodyguards to keep her safe. She wears a chadri, although she is not forced to, because it helps keep her safe because people can't recognize her.

Joya was quick to express her frustration with other members of parliament who she feels are corrupt. Many are, in fact, warlords, drug lords, and criminals. They seized power after the fall of the Taliban and used it for

their own good. She feels that having them control the government is worse than having the Taliban in power.

In a 2007 television interview, Joya said that Afghanistan's parliament was worse than a stable or zoo, comparing warlords and drug lords in power to donkeys. Afterward, the parliament voted to suspend her for three years based on a little-known law that forbids members of parliament from insulting one another. The organization Human Rights Watch has noted that other members frequently criticize one another without being suspended.

Members of parliament also directed the Interior Ministry to restrict Joya's movements within the country. Though she is not allowed to travel outside Afghanistan, she plans to continue leading the struggle for women's rights in Afghanistan.

The lower house, the House of the People, has 249 members. They are all directly elected by the people of their provinces. Members of the House of the People must be at least twenty-five years old, and they must never have been convicted of a crime. Each serves a five-year term. The constitution states that the number of women in the House of the People must be at least twice the number of existing provinces. Currently, Afghanistan has thirty-four provinces so the House of the People must include at least sixty-eight women.

More than 30 percent of the members of the House of the People are women.

The National Assembly creates new laws. Once one house has approved a bill, the other must also approve it. The bill then goes to the president for further approval. The National Assembly also endorses international treaties signed by Afghanistan. Its members approve the president's selections for cabinet ministers. Only the president may declare war or peace, but the National Assembly must approve the declaration.

The first parliament under the current constitution was elected in 2005. Among those elected were former mujahidin, Taliban fighters, and communists. Some bills considered by the first parliament were controversial. Members have debated bills that would forgive their own crimes and war crimes committed by others.

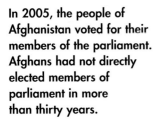

In 2005, the people of Afghanistan voted for their members of the parliament. Afghans had not directly elected members of parliament in more than thirty years.

Hamid Karzai (left) was sworn in as president of Afghanistan in December 2004.

The Judicial Branch

Afghanistan's judicial branch consists of the Supreme Court, appeal courts, and high courts. The Supreme Court has nine members, who are appointed by the president and approved by the House of the People. They serve for a single ten-year term.

The Loya Jirga

The loya jirga meets only for specific reasons. It consists of members of the National Assembly along with the chairpersons of provincial and district councils. It meets to make changes to the constitution, to prosecute the president for serious crimes, or to decide important issues for the country, such as independence and threats to the country's territory.

Kabul: Did You Know This?

Kabul has been Afghanistan's capital since 1776. It is Afghanistan's largest city and the nation's center of culture and finance. Kabul's history mirrors that of the country—it has been around for more than three thousand years, and during that time it has been destroyed by marauding armies and rebuilt, only to be destroyed once again. Mongols, Persians, the Soviet Union, the Taliban—all have been in control of Kabul at various times in history. Though the city was once known for its interesting architecture, much of it is now in ruins from years of war.

Still, some amazing features remain. The Kabul Museum holds many treasures, some dating back to the days before Islam. Much was stolen during the years of chaos in the 1990s, and the building suffered severe damage. The Kabul Zoo has also suffered from the fighting, but it is trying to rebuild with help from zoos around the world.

The old part of Kabul is filled with bazaars where trading goes on much as it has for centuries. But the city is also home to Kabul City Center, Afghanistan's first modern indoor shopping mall.

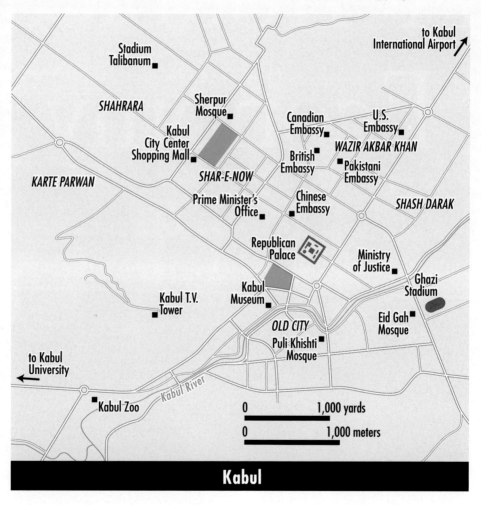

Kabul

A Troubled Economy

AFGHANISTAN IS ONE OF THE POOREST COUNTRIES IN the world. Each citizen earned an average of US$293 in 2006. Many Afghans do not have adequate housing, education, and health care. There are shortages of jobs, clean water, and electricity.

About 40 percent of Afghans who want jobs are unable to find them. Around 80 percent of those who do have jobs are employed in agriculture. Another 10 percent work in industry, and 10 percent in services.

Opposite: **Afghanistan is one of the poorest nations on the planet.**

Desperate Afghans have moved into this devastated building in Kabul.

In 2005, Afghanistan's gross domestic product—the total value of goods and services produced in the country that year—was about US$5.9 billion. (The United States, in contrast, had a GDP of US$12.4 trillion in 2005.) The illegal drug trade brought another US$2.7 billion into the Afghan economy. Drug money, along with financial aid from other nations, makes up a large chunk of Afghanistan's economy.

Agriculture

Agriculture makes up the largest part of Afghanistan's legal economy. It accounts for about 38 percent of the country's income. Today, only about 6 percent of the land in Afghanistan is farmed. Until the fighting of recent decades, 12 percent was suitable for farming. But unexploded land mines, pollution, and craters left behind by bombs have ruined much of the land.

Unexploded land mines are a danger in many parts of Afghanistan. Flags indicate whether an area is safe or not.

It is difficult to make a living farming in Afghanistan. Drought has gripped the country in recent years, and there is little irrigation. Many farmers depend on melting snow and spring rains to water their crops. They lack access to modern farm machinery and soil-enriching fertilizers.

Many Afghan farmers use animals to plow the land.

Wheat and other cereal grains form the largest part of Afghanistan's agricultural economy, but decades of war and years of severe drought crippled their production. Afghanistan must produce 6 million tons (5.4 million metric tons) of cereals each year just to feed its own people. In 2006, the total cereal production was 4.8 million tons (4.4 million metric tons). Many farmers lost 70 to 80 percent of their crops because of the lack of rain. As many as 6.5 million Afghans face serious food shortages because of the loss.

What Afghanistan Grows and Mines

Agriculture

Wheat (2006)	3.37 million metric tons
Timber (2003)	2,858 metric tons

Mning

Natural gas (2003)	50 million cubic meters
Coal (2005)	200,000 metric tons
Quarried stone (2004)	2.7 million cubic meters
Sand (2004)	500,000 cubic meters

Afghanistan is trying to get its cement factories up and running again.

Manufacturing and Trade

Another economic problem facing Afghanistan is a lack of factories to produce necessary goods. The nation's factories were damaged and neglected during earlier decades of war. Today, most of Afghanistan's cement plants sit idle. The country fills its need for cement by buying millions of dollars worth of it each year from Pakistan, where cement factories are expanding to meet the Afghan demand. The same problem exists with textiles and other goods.

Afghanistan's trade deficit with Pakistan was about US$1 billion in 2006. That means that Afghanistan purchased goods worth US$1 billion more than it sold to Pakistan. Afghanistan also has large trade deficits with other countries, including Iran and China. Its total trade deficit is about US$4 billion each year. If Afghan factories were rebuilt, that money could stay in the country and pay for jobs for Afghans.

Most of the country's exports are agricultural products such as fruit and nuts. Afghanistan also exports handwoven carpets, wool, cotton, and animal hides and pelts. Soap, furniture, shoes, and some textiles are among the nation's main manufactured products.

Afghanistan's Currency

The basic unit of currency in Afghanistan is the Afghani. It is divided into 100 puls. As of 2007, US$1 equaled 49 Afghanis, and 1 Afghani equaled about 2¢ in U.S. currency.

Afghani paper money comes in several denominations, including 1, 2, 5, 10, 50, and 500 Afghanis. All the bills include images of Afghan scenes. The 1,000-Afghani bill is colored orange and mauve and displays an image of the Blue Mosque in Mazar-i Sharif.

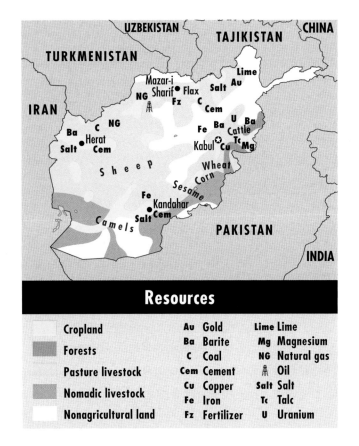

UZBEKISTAN
TAJIKISTAN
CHINA
TURKMENISTAN
IRAN

Mazar-i
Sharif ● Flax
NG
Fz
Lime
Au
Salt
C
Cem
C NG
Ba C
Salt Herat
Cem
Fe
Ba U Ba
Cattle
Kabul ✪ Cu Tc Mg

S h e e p
Wheat
Corn
Sesame
Fe
Kandahar
Salt Cem
C a m e l s

PAKISTAN

INDIA

Resources

▢	Cropland	Au	Gold	Lime	Lime
▨	Forests	Ba	Barite	Mg	Magnesium
▢	Pasture livestock	C	Coal	NG	Natural gas
▨	Nomadic livestock	Cem	Cement	⛽	Oil
▢	Nonagricultural land	Cu	Copper	Salt	Salt
		Fe	Iron	Tc	Talc
		Fz	Fertilizer	U	Uranium

Afghanistan's most important natural resource is natural gas. It was first mined there in 1967, and production reached its peak in the 1980s. Today, gas production has dropped to only about 10 percent of 1980 levels. Other important natural resources in Afghanistan include coal, copper, iron ore, and salt.

The Illegal Drug Trade

For poor Afghans living in rural areas, one of the best ways to earn money is by growing opium poppies. Opium is a drug made from poppy plants, which grow easily in Afghanistan. Opium is used to make heroin, a powerful illegal drug, and some legal medicines. Afghan farmers can earn about ten times more planting poppies than they can by producing legal crops. Some opium profits go to the Taliban, who are pushing the illegal trade to help fund their war.

Opium production requires a lot of labor, so it provides reliable, though illegal, work for many Afghans. It has been estimated that 1.7 million Afghans work in opium production. In 2007, about 9,000 tons (8,200 metric tons) of opium was produced in Afghanistan, enough to make 900 tons (820 metric tons) of heroin. Opium production brought

US$3 billion into the country in 2006, a 60 percent increase over the previous year. Afghanistan produces some 90 percent of the world's opium.

Poppies have been grown in Afghanistan for more than two thousand years. Even then, opium was used as a medicine.

Though most of the opium is exported to other parts of the world, addiction is a growing problem in Afghanistan. In 2006, an estimated 920,000 Afghans were addicted to opium and other drugs.

The Afghan government and other organizations have set up programs to help poppy farmers find other jobs. These programs have not been very successful, however. Few things grow as well in Afghanistan as poppies, and few jobs pay as well as the illegal drug trade. So the problem continues.

From Friend to Brother

THERE IS AN OLD AFGHAN SAYING: "ONE DAY YOU SEE A friend. The next day you see a brother." The saying points out how quickly simple friendships can grow into close relationships. It's a good introduction to the personality of many Afghans. They have a reputation for being warm, generous, and trustworthy, even to those they've just met.

Opposite: **Friendships develop quickly among Afghans.**

Many People, One Nation

Many different ethnic groups make up Afghanistan. These ethnic groups emerged over the centuries as different peoples crossed the land. Some settled in certain areas, while others intermingled with those already there. Greeks, Arabs, Turks, Mongols, and others contributed to the mixing of backgrounds.

Afghanistan's Ethnic Groups

Pashtun	42%
Tajik	27%
Hazara	9%
Uzbek	9%
Other	13%

Carts and cars mingle in many parts of Afghanistan.

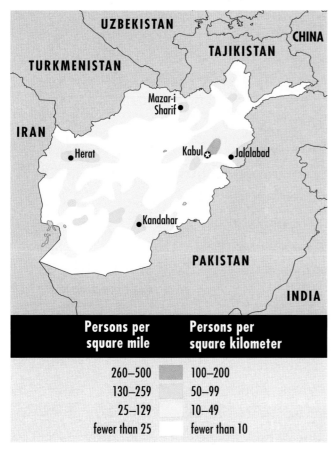

Persons per square mile		Persons per square kilometer
260–500		100–200
130–259		50–99
25–129		10–49
fewer than 25		fewer than 10

These various peoples did not meld quickly into one national identity when Afghanistan came into being. Instead, distinct ethnic groups remained. These groups have remained separate over the years because of the country's rugged geography. The mountains and deserts make travel difficult and sometimes dangerous.

Many Afghans are more loyal to their tribe than to their country. The largest ethnic groups are the Pashtuns and the Tajiks, followed by the Hazaras and the Uzbeks. Afghanistan is also home to a number of smaller ethnic groups.

Pashtuns are the largest ethnic group in Afghanistan and the second largest in Pakistan.

The Pashtuns

Pashtuns make up more than 40 percent of Afghanistan's population. Most, but not all, live in the southern and eastern parts of the country. A large Pashtun population also lives across the border in Pakistan. Though the Pashtuns live in two separate countries, most have strong loyalties to each other, even when their countries are at odds.

The Pashtuns have a strong code of honor, *pashtunwali*, which has been adopted by other Afghans. Though unwritten, pashtunwali directs much of the lives of Pashtuns. It stresses loyalty, courage, hospitality, morality, and honor. Disputes that arise over property or injury are often taken up by entire families. If left unresolved, these disagreements between families may go on for decades.

Though some Pashtuns are nomadic, most are farmers who make their homes in one place. Others are artists and merchants. Pashtuns play a large role in Afghan politics. Hamid Karzai, the president of Afghanistan, is a Pashtun.

A Pashtun girl herds sheep.

Almost all Tajiks are Sunni Muslims.

The Tajiks and the Hazaras

The Tajiks are the second-largest ethnic group in Afghanistan, making up about one-quarter of the population. Tajiks tend to maintain close family ties. Most live in small towns or on farms in the fertile eastern valleys that lie both north and south of the Hindu Kush. In these areas, they grow some of Afghanistan's finest nuts, fruits, and vegetables. Some city-dwelling Tajiks work as craftsmen and traders. In Kabul, a number work in government service, though Tajiks are not dominant at the top levels of politics.

The Hazaras are descended from Mongol warriors. They are closely related to the people of nearby Tajikistan. Most live in Hazarajat, a mountainous region in central Afghanistan. There, they build walled cities and homes from mud and stone. Most Hazaras are farmers and sheep herders.

Hazara women work outside their mud and stone homes. More than three million Hazaras live in Afghanistan.

Afghanistan's Largest Cities

Kabul	2,536,300
Kandahar	316,800
Herat	249,000
Mazar-i Sharif	183,000
Jalalabad	168,600

The Turkic group consists of tribes in Afghanistan that are descended from central Asian Turks, who made their way through Afghanistan in the seventh century. The largest of these groups is the Uzbeks. They are related to the people from one of Afghanistan's neighbors to the north, Uzbekistan. The name *Uzbekistan* means "Land of Uzbeks." Uzbeks live on both sides of that border. Most are farmers and herders. Some are craftspeople famous for their carpets and jewelry.

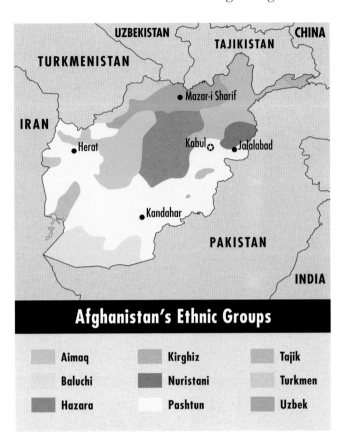

Afghanistan's Ethnic Groups

- Aimaq
- Baluchi
- Hazara
- Kirghiz
- Nuristani
- Pashtun
- Tajik
- Turkmen
- Uzbek

Other Turkic groups include the Turkmen and the Kirghiz. The Turkmen live in the north, on the southern banks of the Amu Darya. They work mostly as farmers. The Kirghiz people came to Afghanistan from Russia. Nomadic Kirghiz live high in the Hindu Kush and the Wakhan Corridor. They herd yaks and live in collapsible, dome-shaped felt tents called *yurts*.

Because their homelands are remote, the Kirghiz are isolated from other Afghans. Many Kirghiz were forced off their land during the Soviet invasion and resettled in Turkey.

Among the other ethnic groups are the Nuristanis, the Aimaqs, and the Baluchis. Before the Soviet invasion, the

Afghan government made an effort to have the various ethnic groups represented proportionally within the national government. Since the end of the last civil war and again since the fall of the Taliban, some ethnic groups have tried to increase their power. This has resulted in violence.

Policemen try to control scuffles in a crowd in Kabul.

From Friend to Brother **87**

Many women in Afghanistan wear chadris. Afghan chadris are typically blue.

Women in Afghanistan

Many factors affect how women in Afghanistan live. The path a woman takes depends on her ethnicity, her financial and educational level, and her family's observance of traditional ways.

The most traditional women in Afghanistan practice *purdah*, staying separate from society at large. They spend most of their lives in their homes, moving from being daughters to being wives and mothers. Their duties are strictly domestic. They cook, clean, and take care of their families. When they do go outside the home, they are always fully covered in a chadri, which is sometimes called a *burqa*. These floor-length cloth coverings can be hot and heavy. They have only a small mesh hole to see through, which makes walking a challenge.

Purdah was the traditional lifestyle for Afghan women. Then, in 1959, Zahir Shah ruled that women no longer needed to practice purdah. They could go out in public without being covered. Some women, especially those living in cities, did just that. They became educated and had careers. The role of women in Afghan society changed quickly.

By the mid-1990s, women held nearly half of all professional positions in Afghanistan. They were doctors and teachers, scientists and lawyers. But in 1996, the Taliban came to power. They imposed strict regulations on the whole of society, but particularly on women. School became off-limits for girls, and women again had to remain in the home, except for on rare occasions. Women had to be completely covered when they went outside. They could be beaten if their bare ankles showed when they walked. They wore soft shoes because it was illegal for their heels to click. They could not leave home without being accompanied by a male relative. Even talking to another man in public was forbidden. Those caught disobeying the rules faced severe penalties, often a public beating or stoning.

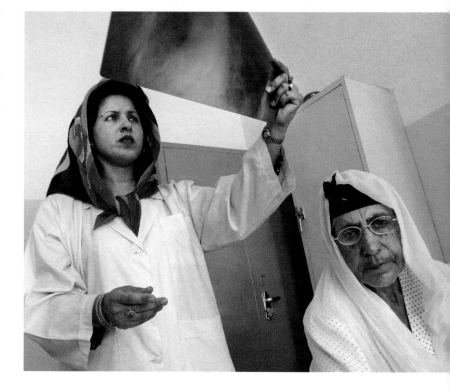

A doctor studies a patient's X-rays at a hospital in Kabul. Female doctors were forced to quit work during the Taliban years.

After the Taliban were overthrown in December 2001, women were freed from the restrictions the Taliban had imposed. But many women were afraid to enjoy their new-found freedom because the punishments under the Taliban had been so severe. Also, many of the men who took over the country treated women the same way the Taliban did. Today, with the Taliban once again gaining strength, many women still carefully observe the restrictions for their own safety.

The Revolutionary Association of the Women of Afghanistan

The Revolutionary Association of the Women of Afghanistan (RAWA) is an organization of Afghan women that formed in 1977 to fight for human rights and social justice. Its members work for democracy, and in more recent years, they have struggled against the religious fundamentalism represented by the Taliban and other conservative rulers. Today, RAWA opposes the antiwoman policies and behavior of those who lead the country.

It can be dangerous to speak for women's rights in Afghanistan. RAWA's founder, a young woman named Meena, was assassinated in 1987.

Refugees

In recent decades, many Afghans have left their country to escape war and poverty. It is estimated that Afghans make up 23 percent of all the refugees in the world. About three million Afghan refugees live in Iran and Pakistan. Both countries are pushing the Afghan refugees out. When refugees go home, they are usually unable to find work or a decent place to live, adding to the poverty in Afghanistan.

More than thirty different languages are spoken in Afghanistan. Many people speak more than one language.

Language

Afghanistan has two official languages, Dari and Pashto. About 50 percent of Afghans speak Dari, a dialect of Persian, which is the language spoken in Iran. (A few other Persian dialects, such as Tajik, are also spoken in Afghanistan.) Dari is usually used in Afghanistan's large, urban areas, especially for business and government.

Pashto is spoken by Pashtuns and others. More than 35 percent of Afghanistan's population speaks Pashto. This language is related to Bactrian, a language spoken in northern

Common Terms in Dari and Pashto

Dari	Pashto	English
salam aleikum	as-salam aleikum	hello
khoda hafez	da khoday-pe-aman	good-bye
lotfan	lutfan	please
tashakor	tashakor	thank you
bale	ho	yes
nay	na	no

Afghanistan in ancient times. But Pashto has also been heavily influenced by other languages. Some Pashto words come from Arabic and classical Greek, the languages of peoples who once controlled Afghanistan.

Many Afghans speak two languages. While all Pashtuns are expected to be fluent in Pashto, for example, many also speak Dari, especially those living in cities. English is also frequently spoken in Afghan cities.

Both Pashto and Dari are written in Arabic script. The Arabic alphabet has twenty-eight letters. Words are written from right to left—the opposite of English—in a beautiful flowing script.

Pashto and Dari are written using the Arabic alphabet.

From Friend to Brother **93**

Putting Islam into Action

"THERE IS NO GOD BUT GOD, AND MUHAMMAD IS THE messenger of God." This is the *shahada*, the Muslim profession of faith. Nearly every adult Afghan has uttered those words, since 99 percent of Afghans are Muslims, or followers of Islam, the country's official religion. The remaining 1 percent are mainly Hindus, Sikhs, and Jews.

The word *Islam* is taken from the Arabic word *aslama*, which means "submission or surrender to God's will." Life for Afghans revolves around Islam. Their daily activities, their frequent prayers, and the respect they show to others are all ways of putting their faith into action.

Opposite: **An old man prays at a mosque. Muslims pray five times a day.**

Men bow in prayer at a mosque in Kabul. People must remove their shoes before entering a mosque.

Afghanistan's Religions

Islam	99%
Other	1%

The History of Islam

The Prophet Muhammad was born in Mecca, now part of Saudi Arabia, in A.D. 570. Muslims believe that when Muhammad was about forty years old, he was visited by the archangel Gabriel. The angel brought Muhammad messages from God, revealing how people should live, what they should believe, and how they should worship. Most important was the message that there was only one god. These revelations, which took place over the next twenty-two years, were recorded in a book called the Qur'an. The Qur'an is the Muslims' holy book, which they believe holds the exact words of God, whom Muslims call Allah.

Muslims typically sit on the ground when they read the Qur'an.

In 613, Muhammad began to preach, telling others about his visions. When Muhammad first shared his message in Mecca, it was not well received. He attracted only a few dozen followers. Meccans already had their own beliefs and practices, and most were furious with Muhammad for attacking the gods they worshipped. Muhammad's life was threatened, and he left Mecca. Muhammad and his followers moved to the town of Medina, which is also in what is now Saudi Arabia. Their journey, made in 622, is known as the *Hijra*, or migration, and marks the beginning of the Islamic calendar.

In Medina, people were much more open to Muhammad's teachings. Within a few years, he had thousands of followers. Muhammad died in 632, but Islam continued to thrive. His successors were known as *caliphs*.

In 642, Arab armies brought Islam to what is now Afghanistan, and gradually the faith moved eastward. By the early 700s, Islam had spread throughout the area that is now Afghanistan.

Islam Splits

There are two main sects, or groups, of Muslims, the Shi'is and the Sunnis. Islam split into these two sects shortly after Muhammad died, when disagreement arose over who should become the caliph, Muhammad's successor. The two leading contenders were Abu Bakr, the father of Muhammad's second wife, and Ali, Muhammad's cousin and son-in-law. Abu Bakr's supporters finally got their man into the role of the first caliph. Ali became the fourth caliph.

The Five Pillars of Islam

The most important practices that Muslims must follow are called the Five Pillars of Islam.

The first pillar is the *shahada*, or declaration of faith. It requires that Muslims say, "There is no god but God, and Muhammad is the messenger of God."

The second pillar is *salat*, the requirement to pray five times daily—at dawn, midday, midafternoon, and sunset, and in the evening before going to bed. The noon prayer on Fridays is usually done in a mosque. At other times, the prayers take place anywhere. Muslims must purify themselves by washing their faces, necks, hands, arms, and feet before praying. Then they kneel, bowing their heads to the ground as a way of showing submission to Allah. They face the holy city of Mecca while praying.

The third pillar, *zakat*, requires that believers give alms, or donations to the poor (above). Muslims are expected to give 2.5 percent of their income, but if they can afford to give more and do so, it is considered a very good deed.

During the holy month of Ramadan, the ninth month of the Islamic calendar, Muslims observe the fourth pillar, *sawm*, or fasting. Pregnant women, travelers, and old and young people don't need to observe this rule. Everyone else abstains from eating, drinking, and smoking during daylight hours. The Ramadan fast is supposed to instill in Muslims a sense of devotion, willpower, moderation, maturity, and unity.

The final pillar, *hajj*, requires that all Muslims make a pilgrimage to Mecca at least once in their lifetime, if possible. During the hajj, pilgrims wear white robes and pray at the Great Mosque in Mecca. Millions of Muslims take part in the hajj each year, making it the world's largest annual convention of faith.

Ali's supporters continued to believe that he was the legitimate successor of Muhammad. They were called *Shi'at 'Ali*, or "Followers of Ali." Today, they are known as Shi'is. They believe that the true leader of Islam should be a direct descendant of Muhammad. Sunnis accept the authority of the caliphs who succeeded Muhammad over the centuries.

In Afghanistan, 84 percent of Muslims are Sunnis. This is about the same percentage as in the Middle East. Most Afghan Shi'is are members of the Hazara ethnic group.

A Shi'i Muslim prays at his home in Kabul.

Islam in Afghanistan

Reading the Qur'an is an important part of Islam. Here, children learn to read the Qur'an at a mosque in Kabul.

There are some fifteen thousand mosques in Afghanistan, one in almost every village and many in each large city. Each mosque is headed by a mullah. The job of a mullah includes leading prayers, delivering a weekly sermon, and performing weddings and funerals. The mullah also runs the Muslim school in each community, where young boys learn basic reading, writing, and arithmetic and study the Qur'an.

Mullah Omar

Mullah Omar, leader of the Taliban in Afghanistan, is also a religious leader who goes by the title *Amir al-Mu'minin*, or "Commander of the Faithful," a title used by the early caliphs. This title was bestowed on Mullah Omar by his cheering Taliban supporters in 1996, when he appeared in Kandahar wrapped in a cloak said to have belonged to the Prophet Muhammad.

An ethnic Pashtun, Mullah Omar was born in 1959 near Kandahar to a poor family. When the Soviets invaded Afghanistan, he joined the mujahidin. A fierce fighter, he was seriously wounded four times, once losing an eye in an explosion. After becoming disabled, he studied to become a mullah. Known for his devotion to pure Islam, he led a religious school outside of Kandahar.

Omar was shocked at the lawless behavior—rape, murder, looting—he saw among the mujahidin. He decided to demand that his followers practice strict rules of fundamentalist Islam. His goal was to create a perfect Muslim state. Many people, eager to be rid of crime, were happy to follow his orders. This was the beginning of the Taliban.

When the Taliban took power in Afghanistan in 1996, Mullah Omar became the country's leader and developed close ties with Osama bin Laden. When the Taliban were overthrown in 2001, Mullah Omar went into hiding. He is still at large. Experts believe he lives in the Pashtun region that straddles the border between Afghanistan and Pakistan.

Afghan Muslims, like Muslims everywhere, strive to make a pilgrimage to Mecca during their lives. But in Afghanistan, Muslims also make smaller pilgrimages. Throughout the country, lesser shrines honor important people from the country's past, such as teachers, poets, and heroes. Some of these shrines are elaborately decorated tombs, while others are simply mounds of dirt marking a grave. Many people make pilgrimages to these shrines, asking for blessings.

The Blue Mosque

The Blue Mosque in Mazar-i Sharif is one of the world's most important mosques and a leading pilgrimage destination. Many Shi'i Muslims believe that Ali, Muhammad's cousin and son-in-law, is buried there. Shi'is consider Ali to be Muhammad's rightful successor. People travel for hundreds of miles to pray at the Blue Mosque. It is decorated with beautiful yellow and blue mosaic tiles in ornate geometric and floral patterns.

Islam helps hold together the various tribes and ethnic groups in Afghanistan, providing strict codes of behavior and social rules. Afghans follow the shar'ia, the body of laws based on the Qur'an and judges' decisions over time. Shar'ia law prohibits Muslims from killing, stealing, lying, and drinking alcohol. They are instructed to dress and behave modestly, to be charitable, and to be just in their dealings. Muslims are not allowed to eat pork or the meat of any animal that has died of natural causes. Muslim men may marry Christian, Jewish, or Muslim women, but Muslim women are allowed to marry only Muslim men. In each community, shar'ia law is administered by a religious judge, called a *qadi*.

Muslims believe the Qur'an includes all the messages that God sent to Muhammad.

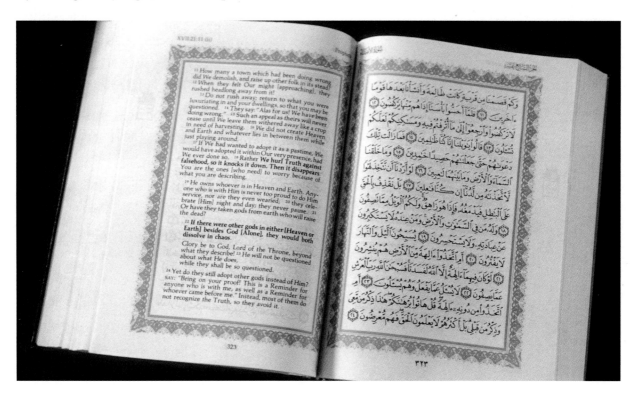

The Islamic Calendar

The Islamic calendar is sometimes called the hijri calendar because it begins with the year that Muhammad began the hijra, his journey from Mecca to Medina. The Islamic calendar is based on phases of the Moon. In this type of calendar, one month is the period of time between two new moons and one year is 354 days. The Gregorian calendar, which is commonly used in the Western world, is based on the solar year, which has 365 days. Afghans typically use the Gregorian calendar for scheduling business meetings and other regular events. Religious holidays are based on the Islamic calendar. The Islamic calendar is eleven days shorter than the Gregorian, so each year Muslim holidays fall on different days of the Gregorian calendar.

Religious Holidays

Muslims in Afghanistan observe several holy days and times during the year. During the month of Ramadan, Muslims fast from sunrise to sunset. In Kabul, a loud cannon blast wakes everyone up early, so they have time to eat an early meal, called *sahari*, before the sun comes up. Each evening at sunset, families come together for the meal that breaks the fast, called *iftar*. Nighttime is busy for Afghans during Ramadan because that is when they get together to socialize and conduct business.

Following Ramadan, Afghans observe ʻId al-Fitr. During this joyful three-day celebration, families get together for delicious feasts. They wear new clothing, buy gifts for their children, and donate money to the poor.

ʻId al-Adha, or the Feast of Sacrifice, takes place each year at the end of the hajj. It honors the prophet Abraham's readiness to obey God and sacrifice his only son, Isaac. At the last moment, God told him to sacrifice a sheep instead. Today, Afghans sacrifice a sheep, prepare the meat, and keep some of the meat for a feast for themselves. They share the rest with friends and poor people.

The Islamic New Year is celebrated on the first day of *Muharram*, the first month of the Islamic calendar. Families gather to share a meal, but it is not an extravagant event. The Prophet's birthday, *Mawlud al-Nabi*, is a lively celebration with feasting and dancing late into the night. It takes place during the third month of the Islamic calendar, *Rabi' al-Awwal*.

Young girls feast on fruit during 'Id al Fitr.

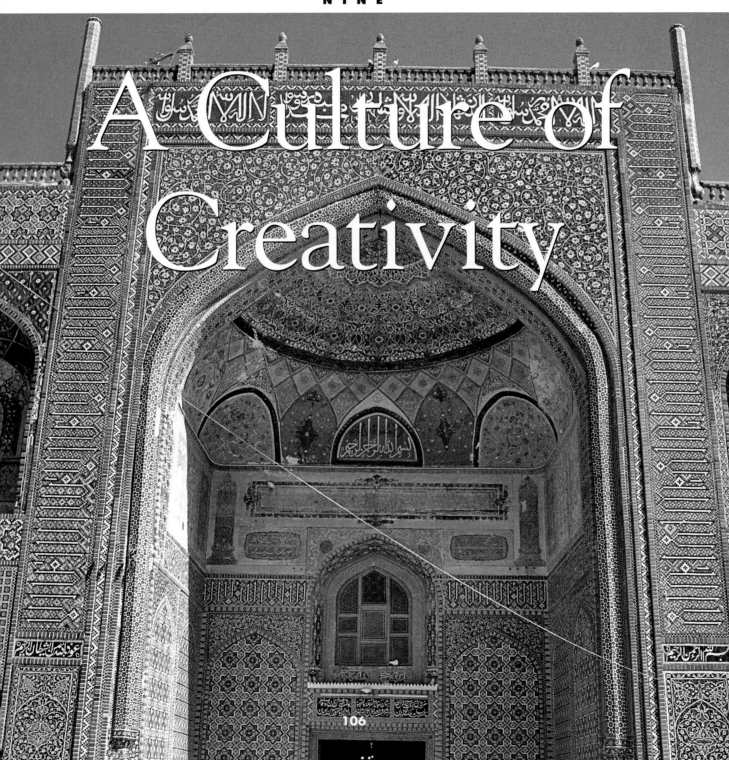

A Culture of Creativity

Afghanistan's rich culture is the result of thousands of years of human creativity. Influences have come from many directions—from the nation's different ethnic groups, from foreign invaders, from traders passing through, and from Islam.

Opposite: **Many mosques in Afghanistan feature intricate tile work.**

Poetry

Poetry is the most common form of literature in Afghanistan. The country is often called the "nation of poets." Through the years, Afghans have been encouraged to memorize verse. When the Taliban ruled, it was illegal to keep copies of poems, so knowing them by heart became even more important. Many Afghans write their own poems, putting their hopes, joys, sorrows, and frustrations into their work.

Famous Afghan poets include Rabi'a Balkhi, a woman who lived in the ninth century and wrote in Persian. Mawlana Jalal al-Din al-Rumi, born in Balkh in 1207, is perhaps the greatest mystical poet of all time. He too wrote in Persian, and his work has been translated into many languages. The poems of both Balkhi and Rumi often speak of love and war. Rumi's poetry also describes finding Allah in everyday life—in people and in nature. In the seventeenth century, Khushal Khan Khattak wrote

Mawlana Jalal al-Din al-Rumi is considered one of the greatest poets ever to write in the Persian language.

poems in Pashto that offered guidance on how to live a proper life. Today, he is considered the national poet of Afghanistan.

A more modern poet was Khalilullah Khalili (1907–1987), a government official, professor of literature, and ambassador to various countries, whose poems are much loved today.

Art

Islamic art is distinctive because it rarely depicts humans, animals, or plants. Because Allah is thought of as the sole creator of life, many Muslims believe that it would be trespassing on his role to make an image of a life-form. Instead, Islamic art employs intricate geometric patterns and designs. Generally, people, plants, or animals found in Islamic art are highly stylized and abstract, far from reality.

The Blue Mosque is one of Afghanistan's artistic treasures.

One of Afghanistan's best examples of Islamic art is the Blue Mosque in Mazar-i Sharif. The mosque is covered with tiles in various shades of blue that depict trailing vines and leaves. It was built during the Great Timurid Era (1369–1504), when many mosques were constructed. The beautiful Friday Mosque in Herat was also built then.

The Great Timurid Era was a particularly good time for the arts in Afghanistan. The Timurid leaders helped support artists, especially those practicing a style of miniature painting that flourished in Herat.

Artists today continue to create lovely copperwork and intricate carpets. But the almost constant violence in recent decades has prevented many artists from developing their craft in the open.

Afghanistan is famous for its beautiful carpets.

Music and Dance

Since 2001, when the Taliban's ban on music and dancing was lifted, traditional music and folk singing have enjoyed renewed popularity. Music accompanies many weddings,

The Kabul Museum

The Kabul Museum, also known as the Afghan National Museum, once held one of central Asia's finest collections of ancient artifacts. Founded in the 1920s, it grew to have more than one hundred thousand items, including ancient coins and treasured objects made of gold and ivory. But in 1993, the museum was bombed. Many objects were destroyed. In the aftermath, others were stolen and sold to collectors around the world.

Just a few years later, some 1,400 pieces still remaining in the museum were sent to Switzerland for safekeeping. In a rare moment of cooperation, Taliban leaders and their Northern Alliance opponents asked that the items be shipped out. The Taliban were concerned that their more hard-line members would destroy the pieces, and in doing so, erase a part of Afghanistan's history. Among the pieces saved was a ceremonial glass object used by Alexander the Great. The treasures from the Kabul Museum were returned to Afghanistan in March 2007. Some damaged pieces, such as this statue, have been reconstructed and are again on display.

religious holidays, and other celebrations. The *attan*, the national dance of Afghanistan, is particularly popular. It is usually performed by men, though women may take part as well. Groups, sometimes numbering more than a hundred, dance in a circle. Their movements build in intensity and speed along with the beat of the music. Attans sometimes last a half hour or more. They are physically demanding and often end with all the dancers on the ground, exhausted.

Music accompanying the attan is usually provided by a *dhol*, or a double-headed barrel drum. Other popular traditional instruments include the *toola*, a wooden flute, and an instrument with eighteen strings known as the *robab*.

Men dance the attan, Afghanistan's national dance. When the Taliban were in power, dancing was forbidden.

Afghan men attend a funeral service.

Birth and Death Customs

Afghan ceremonies commemorate both the beginning and the end of life on earth. Great celebrations follow the birth of a baby, especially if it is a boy. In some family traditions, the celebration lasts three days. In wealthy families, it goes on for ten. During this time, a local mullah visits the family. He whispers to the baby its name and a Muslim blessing: *Allahu akbar* ("God is great").

Ceremonies also mark the end of life. Muslims believe that people join Allah when they die. The body is bathed a final time by relatives, a mullah offers final prayers, and the body is covered with a white sheet. It is buried on its right side, facing the holy city of Mecca. Family members say prayers for the deceased every Thursday night for a year.

Ahmad Zahir

Years after his death in a car accident, Ahmad Zahir remains one of Afghanistan's most beloved musicians. Born in 1946, Zahir began performing while he was young. Zahir listened to music from around the world and brought a variety of rhythms into his work, making his music unlike any that Afghans had heard before. Zahir understood the need capture the audience's attention with emotion and body movement. Though his political songs were banned by the government, he was wildly popular with his fellow Afghans. He died in 1979, but many people still listen to his music.

Marriage Customs

Weddings prompt big celebrations in Afghanistan. Family and friends from near and far gather for the event, which features feasting and music.

Most marriages are arranged. It's common for teenagers to marry members of their own extended family or people from the same tribe or ethnic background. Typically, when a girl is a young teen, the older women in her family start seeking a possible husband for her. They meet female relatives of young men, looking for someone whose family is well respected, someone who is strong, brave, and financially secure. The groom's relatives want to find a bride who will be hardworking and easygoing. Once the women of both families reach agreement, the men of the family get involved.

Each family makes a contribution. The bride's family provides a dowry, which includes items the couple will need in their home such as pots and pans, dishes, and blankets. The groom's family pays the *mahr*, the bride price. It is a charge for the girl's hand in marriage. The mahr can be money. Sometimes cattle and property are exchanged as well. If a husband should ever divorce his wife, she is supposed to keep the mahr, that is, if it has not already been spent.

The wedding ceremony itself has two parts. First, the bride's father and the groom sign a wedding pact. Then, the bride and groom exchange vows during the ceremony. Afterward, they celebrate with their guests. Men and women enjoy the festivities separately, as is common in most activities in traditional Muslim cultures. Men typically gather in rooms with elaborate rugs and pillows on the floor, while women often sit outside or in a different room in the home.

Fun and Games

Throughout their decades of struggle, Afghans have not forgotten how to laugh and have fun. The Taliban outlawed most sports, but today Afghans are again enjoying a variety of athletic games.

Pahlwani, a sport similar to wrestling, is popular throughout the country. Players compete to knock over their opponent, touching only their body, arms, and clothes but not their legs.

The National Game

Buzkashi, which literally means "grab the goat," is considered Afghanistan's national game. It was invented by nomadic warriors from the north, where it may have come from hunting mountain goats. Traditionally, a beheaded goat was used as the target, but today, it is more likely to be a dead calf.

Teams of ten to twenty men on horseback race toward the animal carcass. A player scoops it up and rushes to get it into a circle in the field, while the opposing team tries to wrestle the carcass away. It can be a dangerous game—the carcass itself can weigh about 150 pounds (70 kg). A rider has to carry it, guide the horse in the right direction, and stay on, all while racing toward the goal.

Buzkashi is played year-round, in the heat, in the rain, and even on snow-covered fields. The large crowds that gather to watch always bring plenty of enthusiasm.

Afghanistan's National Holidays

Nawroz (traditional Iranian New Year)	March 21
Liberation Day	April 18
Revolution Day	April 28
Labor Day	May 1
Afghan Independence Day	August 19

The game can get rough, and sometimes the players' clothes are torn to shreds. The winner must pin his opponent down by his shoulders.

Another Afghan game is played by children on some religious holidays. Two players each have a colorful hard-boiled egg. They knock their eggs together, and the loser is the one whose egg cracks first. The winner keeps both eggs. It sounds simple, but players insist that there is a lot of technique and strategy involved.

Afghans also enjoy sports more familiar in the rest of the world. In 2007, Afghanistan put together its first women's national soccer team. The team, which includes girls in their early teens who would be playing in youth leagues in many countries, traveled to Pakistan for its first international tournament in August 2007. Many of the team members wear head scarves. Most had never played on a full-size field before. Still, the team did well, advancing to the tournament finals, much to the thrill of the Afghan refugees who filled the stands.

Kite Flying

Kite flying has a long tradition in Afghanistan. Children, especially boys, make their own kites using colorful tissue paper pulled tight on a light wooden frame. Many compete in a sport called kite fighting. In kite fighting, the kite string is coated with ground glass. The boys fly their kites, making them swoop into each other and trying to cross the kite

strings. Then they pull the kite in a sawing motion, trying to cut the strings of their competitor's kite.

When the Taliban were in change, they put an end to kite flying. They thought it was too frivolous. Children caught flying kites often faced severe punishment, as did their parents. Since the fall of the Taliban, Afghans have enthusiastically returned to the sport. They hope they won't be forced to say good-bye to kites once again if the Taliban regain power.

Kite flying is one of the most popular pastimes in Afghanistan. On any given day, hundreds of kites soar in the air above Kabul and other cities.

Living Day by Day

116

Girls in Herat make bread in the courtyard of their house.

I N WEALTHIER COUNTRIES, IN PEACEFUL TIMES, MOST PEOPLE do not have to worry much about feeding their families. They don't need to worry about how to get an education, or if they will be cared for when they are old or sick. They take those things for granted. Not so in Afghanistan. There, finding food, education, and health care is a struggle.

Afghan Food

The flavors of several different cultures come together in Afghan cuisine. India has influenced the spices used in Afghan food. The Persian tradition of slow-cooking meat, especially lamb and chicken, along with spinach and mint, shows up frequently on Afghan tables. Afghans also adopted noodles from Mongolian cooking.

Opposite: **An Afghan girl takes a ride on a small Ferris wheel.**

The most common Afghan bread is flat and rectangular. It is often sprinkled with caraway seeds or cumin seeds.

Popular Afghan foods include traditional flatbreads called *lawash* and *naan*; yogurt, onions, and tomatoes; and Afghan walnuts. Rice is often served with *kormas*, savory vegetable mixes containing such ingredients as bell peppers, eggplant, pumpkin, and potato, blended together with yogurt. Favorite seasonings include cardamom, cumin, saffron, coriander, and dill.

Hospitality is central to Afghan culture, and families frequently invite guests to their homes. Guests get a special seat at the head of the room. Traditionally, Afghans eat while seated on pillows placed on thick carpets on the floor. The carpet's center is covered by a thin mat called a *dusterkhan*.

Tables and chairs are becoming more common, however. In the heat of the summer, Afghans might eat outside under the shade of a tree or in the cool night air. All the women and girls of the host family serve the food, while the men chat with their visitors.

Kabeli Pilau

Kabeli pilau is a popular Afghan meal of chicken and rice. It is often offered to guests.

Ingredients

4 tablespoons vegetable oil

2 large onions, sliced

1 teaspoon ground cardamom

2 teaspoons cumin

¼ teaspoon saffron

2 large carrots, sliced into matchsticks

2 pounds chicken, cut into bite-sized pieces

6 cups water

1 pound rice

Salt and pepper to taste

4 ounces raisins

Directions

Heat the vegetable oil in a pan and add the sliced onions. Stir and fry the onions until they are brown. When they are cooked, add cardamom, cumin, and saffron. Remove the onions from the stove, and grind them with the seasonings until a smooth paste is formed. Set aside. Simmer the carrots in a bit of water until tender and set aside.

Heat the chicken and water in a large pan. Bring the water to a boil, and simmer until the meat is cooked. Then remove the chicken and set it aside. Bring the water back to a boil, add the rice, salt, and pepper, and simmer until the rice is cooked, about 20 minutes.

Combine the rice, meat, and onion paste. Stir. Put the mixture into a casserole dish, sprinkle the carrots and raisins over the top, cover, and bake at 300°F for about 45 minutes. Mix lightly, and serve.

Tea, Afghanistan's most common beverage, is offered at the beginning of a meal. It is usually followed by a large platter of rice accompanied by many side dishes such as soups, stews, vegetables, pickles, yogurt, sauces, and bread. Desserts, usually rich puddings, are eaten next, followed by fruits such as grapes, melons, pomegranates, and apricots.

Enormous amounts of food are served to visitors, and guests usually get the best a host can afford. A host will even go without food at a meal to make sure visitors have good things to eat. It would be rude for guests to refuse anything, and they are expected to take second helpings.

Afghan brick makers enjoy tea during a break from work. Afghans typically drink tea throughout the day.

Many women in rural Afghanistan wear chadris. Chadris cover the entire face and have a mesh opening in front of the eyes.

Clothing

Most women in Afghanistan wear clothing similar to women in Western countries, but they're rarely seen in public that way. Many Afghan women wear a chadri over their clothes when they're outside their homes. Chadris cover them from head to toe, leaving only a small mesh opening for their eyes. Most chadris are blue, black, or brown.

Most Afghan men wear loose cotton pants and turbans.

The most typical clothing for Afghan men is the *kameez partoog*, which is loose-fitting cotton pants topped by a thigh-length tunic belted at the waist. A sleeveless vest is usually worn over this. In colder weather, men will also wear a *chupan*, a wool coat that reaches nearly to the ground. Sandals are common footwear in warm weather, or thick wool socks and boots in the winter.

Education

In 2006, about 5 million Afghan children—less than half those eligible—attended school. This number has grown since 2003, when only 3.1 million Afghan children attended school. In 2001, during the Taliban's rule, only about 1 million children went to classes. The government is trying to improve education, but this is difficult as there are not enough teachers or schools.

A teacher gives lessons in an unheated room with no furniture. More than half the schools in Afghanistan have no classrooms.

Afghanistan's Literacy Rate

The literacy rate is the percentage of people over fifteen years old who can read and write.

All Afghans	36%
Afghan males	51%
Afghan females	21%

Many of Afghanistan's existing schools are in disrepair, the legacy of years of war and poverty. More than half have no clean drinking water or toilet facilities. About two million children go to classes where there are no school buildings. Instead, they attend classes in a tent or in the open air. The Afghan government has requested help from other countries to rebuild 7,800 schools across the country. The country also needs to add more than one hundred thousand trained primary school teachers over the next few years in order to have enough teachers to educate the children. This is not likely in a country where teachers are paid only about US$38 per month, less than most teachers could earn at other jobs.

Other problems also keep children out of school. Many families are too poor to pay school fees, buy books, and clothe and feed their children adequately. They need to keep their children at home so the children can work and help provide for the family.

Girls in Afghanistan have an extra challenge getting an education. Only one in five goes to elementary school, and only one in twenty gets a high school education. During the Taliban period, education was forbidden for girls. After the Taliban lost power, girls could go back to school if facilities and teachers were available in their area. But many girls had fallen behind in their studies. They were reluctant to return to classes where they would be taught alongside much younger children. Additionally, many girls are uncomfortable taking

classes along with boys or being taught by male teachers. Less than a third of all teachers are women.

With the Taliban regaining power in parts of the country, girls seeking an education and those teaching them are again in danger. Attacks on schools are on the rise. Dozens of teachers have been killed. In 2006, four teachers in Ghazna were killed by the Taliban because they refused to stop educating girls. The body of one was put on display as a warning to others. The Taliban were also responsible for setting fire to 110 schools throughout Afghanistan in 2006 alone. The schools were accused of offering un-Islamic education.

The situation is less bleak for children born into wealthy families. Major cities have schools. In some of them, girls attend classes and even participate in sports.

Afghan children in major cities are much more likely to attend school than those in the countryside. In some regions of southern Afghanistan, almost no children attend school.

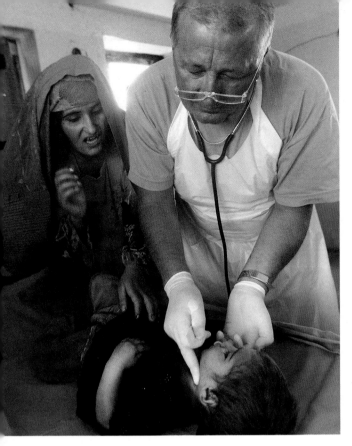

A European doctor examines a sick child in Kabul. About half of Afghan children under the age of five have stunted growth because they do not get enough to eat.

Health Care

Afghanistan has one of the world's least-developed health care systems. Men and women in Afghanistan have an average life expectancy of less than forty-three years. Only about one-eighth of the population has access to safe, clean, drinking water. Because of this, many suffer from illnesses caused by impure water, especially diarrhea, which can be deadly. It's a common Afghan practice to avoid giving much food or liquid to children with diarrhea. But this only puts the child in more danger. Afghans also frequently die of measles, respiratory infections, and malaria, illnesses that can be prevented and treated.

Few Afghans have access to good health care. Medical care is centered in Kabul. Usually, it is provided by foreigners working for international aid organizations. Many rural areas have no hospitals or doctors at all. The country's public health ministry is working to solve this problem. An effort is underway to set up small clinics in rural areas and to have traveling health teams available to treat people living there.

Pregnant women and children in particular do not always get the treatment they need. More than three hundred thousand children under age five in Afghanistan don't get enough to eat, and many suffer from severe malnutrition. The death rate among babies and young children in Afghanistan is among the highest in the world, though it has improved in recent years. In 2001, 165 infants died out of every 1,000 children born. That number had dropped to 135 by 2006.

The main reason for the improvement is that women have had an easier time getting medical care since the Taliban were ousted from power. In 2003, only 5 percent of women saw a doctor while they were pregnant. By 2006, the number had risen to 30 percent. Since 2004, there has been a push to improve health care for children, especially to get them the vaccinations that prevent disease.

Life Goes On

Life presents many challenges to the people of Afghanistan. They must fight to get the same things that people in many other countries take for granted. Many struggle daily just to keep their children fed and healthy. They dream of the day when they can feel safe and the wars will come to an end. That day is not yet here, but the people of Aghanistan refuse to give up.

Young children in the Bamyan Valley of central Afghanistan. About 45 percent of Afghans are less than fifteen years old.

Timeline

Afghan History

Prehistoric people live in the foothills of the Hindu Kush.	**ca. 100,000** B.C.
Farmers gather into small agricultural villages and cities.	**ca. 4000** B.C.
Aryans move into Afghanistan from central Asia.	**ca. 1500** B.C.
Alexander the Great conquers parts of Afghanistan.	**329** B.C.
Buddhism is introduced to Afghanistan.	**304** B.C.
The Kushans take control of Afghanistan.	**130** B.C.
Islam is introduced into Afghanistan.	A.D. **642**
The Samanids conquer Afghanistan.	**920**
The Ghaznavid dynasty begins.	**998**
The Mongols invade Afghanistan.	**1219**
The Great Timurid Era begins.	**1369**
Babur, the founder of the Mughal Empire, conquers Kabul.	**1504**
The Durrani dynasty is founded.	**1747**

World History

2500 B.C.	Egyptians build the pyramids and the Sphinx in Giza.
563 B.C.	The Buddha is born in India.
A.D. **313**	The Roman emperor Constantine legalizes Christianity.
610	The Prophet Muhammad begins preaching a new religion called Islam.
1054	The Eastern (Orthodox) and Western (Roman Catholic) Churches break apart.
1095	The Crusades begin.
1215	King John seals the Magna Carta.
1300s	The Renaissance begins in Italy.
1347	The plague sweeps through Europe.
1453	Ottoman Turks capture Constantinople, conquering the Byzantine Empire.
1492	Columbus arrives in North America.
1500s	Reformers break away from the Catholic Church, and Protestantism is born.
1776	The U.S. Declaration of Independence is signed.
1789	The French Revolution begins.

Afghan History

Dost Muhammad Khan's reign begins.	1826
The First Anglo-Afghan war begins.	1839
The Second Anglo-Afghan war begins.	1878
The Durand Line is drawn, marking the boundary between Afghanistan and India (now Pakistan) through the Hindu Kush.	1893
The Third Anglo-Afghan war is fought.	1919
Afghanistan gains independence from Britain.	1921
Afghanistan's first constitution is written.	1923
Muhammad Zahir Shah begins his 40-year reign.	1933
Mohammad Daoud seizes power.	1973
Daoud is assassinated in the April Revolution.	1978
The Soviet Union invades Afghanistan.	1979
The Soviets withdraw.	1989
The Taliban gain control of Afghanistan.	1996
Al-Qa'ida terrorists, supported by the Taliban, attack New York City and Washington, D.C. In retaliation, U.S. military forces topple the Taliban.	2001
Afghanistan's first democratic elections are held; Hamid Karzai is elected president.	2004
The Taliban begin to regain power.	2006

World History

1865	The American Civil War ends.
1879	The first practical light bulb is invented.
1914	World War I begins.
1917	The Bolshevik Revolution brings communism to Russia.
1929	A worldwide economic depression begins.
1939	World War II begins.
1945	World War II ends.
1957	The Vietnam War begins.
1969	Humans land on the Moon.
1975	The Vietnam War ends.
1989	The Berlin Wall is torn down as communism crumbles in Eastern Europe.
1991	The Soviet Union breaks into separate states.
2001	Terrorists attack the World Trade Center in New York City and the Pentagon in Washington, D.C.

Fast Facts

Official name: Islamic Republic of Afghanistan

Capital: Kabul

Official languages: Dari and Pashto

Kabul

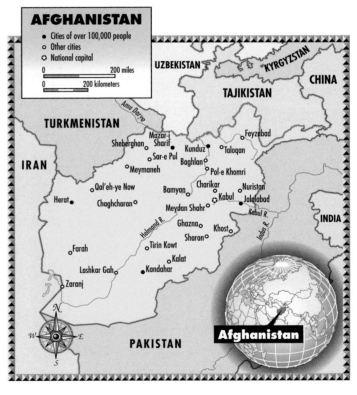

Afghanistan's flag

Band-i Zulfiqar Lake

Official religion:	Islam
Year of founding:	1921
National anthem:	"Milli Tharana" ("National Anthem")
Type of government:	Islamic republic
Chief of state:	President
Head of government:	President
Area:	250,775 square miles (649,504 sq km)
Latitude and longitude of geographic center:	33°00' N, 65°00' E
Bordering countries:	Pakistan to the south and east; Iran to the west; Tajikistan, Turkmenistan, and Uzbekistan to the north; China to the northeast
Highest elevation:	Mount Nowshak, 24,557 feet (7,485 m)
Lowest elevation:	In the Sistan Basin, 1,640 feet (500 m) above sea level
Average temperatures:	In summer, 120°F (49°C) in the south; in winter, −15°F (−26°C) in the mountains
Average precipitation:	12 inches (30 cm)
National population (2007 est.):	31,889,923

Blue Mosque

Currency

Population of largest cities (2006 est.):

Kabul	2,536,300
Kandahar	316,000
Herat	249,000
Mazar-i Sharif	183,000
Jalalabad	168,600

Famous landmarks:

▶ *The Blue Mosque*, Mazar-i Sharif

▶ *The Friday Mosque*, Herat

▶ *Remains of Bamyan Buddhas*, Bamyan

▶ *Babur's Tomb*, Kabul

▶ *Ahmad Mas'ud's Tomb*, Panjshir Valley

Industry: Afghanistan's most important natural resource is natural gas. The largest sector of the country's economy is agriculture. Afghanistan's major crop is wheat, followed by timber, other cereal grains, fruit, and nuts. Illegal opium is one of the country's largest exports.

Currency: The Afghani. In 2007, US$1 equaled 49 Afghanis, and one Afghani equaled about 2¢ in U.S. currency.

System of weights and measures: Metric system

Literacy rate: 36 percent

Schoolchildren

Malalai Joya

Common Afghan words and phrases:

Dari	Pashto	English
salam aleikum	*as-salam aleikum*	hello
khoda hafez	*da khoday-pe-aman*	good-bye
lotfan	*lutfan*	please
tashakor	*tashakor*	thank you
bale	*ho*	yes
nay	*na*	no

Famous people:

Dost Muhammad Khan (1793–1863)
Emir of Afghanistan

Ahmad Shah Abdali Durrani (1723–1773)
Founder of the Durrani dynasty

Malalai Joya (1978–)
Youngest member of Afghanistan's parliament

Hamid Karzai (1957–)
President of Afghanistan

Khushal Khan Khattak (1613–1690)
Poet

Mahmud of Ghazna (971–1030)
Founder of the Ghaznavid dynasty

Ahmad Shah Mas'ud (1953–2001)
Leader of the Northern Alliance

Mullah Omar (1959–)
Leader of the Taliban

Jalal al-Din al-Rumi (1207–1273)
Poet

Muhammad Zahir Shah (1914–2007)
King of Afghanistan

To Find Out More

Books

▶ Akbar, Said Hyder, and Susan Burton. *Come Back to Afghanistan*. New York: Bloomsbury Publishing, 2005.

▶ Boaz, John, ed. *Afghanistan*. San Diego: Greenhaven Press, 2004.

▶ Kazem, Halima. *Afghanistan*. Milwaukee: Gareth Stevens Publishing, 2003.

▶ Parks, Peggy J. *Afghanistan*. San Diego: Blackbirch Press, 2003.

▶ Romano, Amy. *A Historical Atlas of Afghanistan*. New York: Rosen Publishing, 2003.

▶ Stewart, Gail. *Life Under the Taliban*. San Diego: Lucent Books, 2005.

Web Sites

▶ **Afghanistan Online**
www.afghan-web.com
For general information on Afghanistan's history, culture, economy, and more.

▶ **Ariana Media**

www.e-ariana.com

To read current news from
Afghanistan.

▶ **Afghanland.com**

www.afghanland.com

For news, history, and culture of
Afghanistan.

▶ **Revolutionary Association of the**
Women of Afghanistan

www.rawa.org

For information and commentary on
women's rights in Afghanistan.

Embassies and Organizations

▶ **Embassy of Afghanistan in the**
United States
2341 Wyoming Ave. NW
Washington, DC 20008
202/483-6410
www.embassyofafghanistan.org

▶ **Embassy of Afghanistan in Canada**
246 Queen Street, Suite 400
Ottawa, Ontario K1P 5E4
613/563-4223
www.afghanemb-canada.net

Index

Page numbers in *italics* indicate illustrations.

Meet the Author

AFGHANISTAN HAS OFTEN BEEN IN THE HEADLINES IN recent years. On many days, you can open a newspaper and read about events there. But you need to dig deeper to really understand the Afghan people and their country. Why could a group like the Taliban gain power in Afghanistan? Why do Afghan farmers grow the poppies that are used to create the drugs opium and heroin? Why do Afghan women wear long robes known as chadris? These were just some of the questions Terri Willis had when she began working on this book. There were lots of good places to find answers.

When Willis began research for this book, one of the first things she did was look for a source that would both provide a good historical background and whet her appetite for the subject. The book *Come Back to Afghanistan* provided just the entry into the country and its culture that she was looking for. The author is Said Hyder Akbar, who wrote it along with Susan Burton. Akbar's family fled Afghanistan when he was toddler, and he grew up in California. In Afghanistan, Akbar's father had been an important political leader. He returned in 2002, to help rebuild the government. Akbar, still a teenager, spent the summers with his father and was an eyewitness to

many historic events in current Afghanistan. He writes about his experiences with an appreciation for Afghan culture, a keen understanding of Afghan history, and the sensibilities of a California teenager.

After that book got her started, Willis continued her research at her alma mater, the University of Wisconsin–Madison, where the libraries hold many books and documents about Afghanistan. She also found good resources on the Internet. Embassies provided further information. She hopes that after reading this book, young people have a better understanding of the issues behind the headlines about Afghanistan.

Willis has written several other books about the Middle East for the Enchantment of the World series, including *Kuwait*, *Lebanon*, *Qatar*, and *Libya*. She also wrote *Romania*, *Vietnam*, *Venezuela*, and *Democratic Republic of the Congo* for the series. She has a degree in journalism and lives in Cedarburg, Wisconsin, with her husband, Harold, and their daughters, Andrea and Liza.

Photo Credits